More Praise for *The Innovation Paradox*

"Davila and Epstein have done it again. After their very successful first book (co-authored with Rob Shelton), *Making Innovation Work*, they introduce the insightful concept of the Startup Corporation, which combines two seemingly contradictory mindsets and skillsets: the ability of startups to create new business opportunities and the disciplined execution of large corporations to achieve profitable growth. This combination is required if the corporation is to develop the capability for continuously generating innovations. Davila and Epstein take the reader through a framework for creating the Startup Corporation that addresses both tangible factors such as strategy, systems, and incentives and intangible ones such as organizational culture and leadership style. The book is practical and engaging and provides numerous tools for creating an innovative organization."
—S. Ramakrishna Velamuri, Professor of Entrepreneurship and Department Chair (Strategy and Entrepreneurship), China Europe International Business School

"Written by world-class authorities on innovation, product development, and start-up life cycles, this book is a must-read for any entrepreneur. As CEO of a venture-backed startup, I've learned an immense amount from it."
—Sunil Rajaraman, CEO, Scripted.com

"Breakthrough innovation is no longer a mystery—Davila and Epstein have broken the code. Now even the most established organization can come up with disruptive products and services."
—Klaus Peter Müller, Principal, Roland Berger Strategy Consultants GmbH, Germany

"Davila and Epstein have done impressive research to uncover the hidden impediments to innovation present in most established organizations. Their recommendations for overcoming those impediments while preserving existing success are well thought out and very practical."
—Gloria Perrier-Châtelain, Senior Global Director, Digital Marketing Strategy, and Partner, SAP, France

"For the first time, Davila and Epstein offer a solution to the 'startup envy' experienced by so many organizations. They show that, with the right adjustments, innovations can flow from high-rises as well as from garages."
—Bence Andras, Partner, Proventus AG, Switzerland

"Original and thoroughly researched, but pragmatic and accessible, this book will be a vital resource for executives, scholars, and even startups looking to keep the breakthrough ideas coming."
—Soumitra Dutta, Dean, Johnson Graduate School of Management, Cornell University

"Davila and Epstein have crushed the prevailing mindset that business units, operational excellence, and traditional approaches to innovation can deliver sustained growth. *The Innovation Paradox* makes it abundantly clear that every company needs to capture and operationalize a startup's entrepreneurial zeal and clock speed to successfully drive growth through innovation. Building and balancing the traditional and startup operating models is the top item for every company's growth agenda."

   —Robert Shelton, coauthor of *Making Innovation Work* and designated an Innovation
   Champion by the World Economic Forum

"Davila and Epstein solve the perennial mystery that has puzzled many corporate leaders: what are the forces inside large companies that prevent them from developing breakthrough innovations? This book provides an insightful framework for diagnosing those forces and tools for overcoming organizational inertia to implement processes that result in breakthroughs."

   —Steven C. Currall, Dean and Professor of Management, Graduate School of
   Management, University of California, Davis, and coauthor of *Organized Innovation*

"*The Innovation Paradox* sheds light on how large corporations can successfully innovate while creating shareholder value. The authors wisely differentiate between breakthrough innovation and incremental innovation. The book informs the reader on how different corporate cultures and management styles play a key role in being successful at different points of the innovation spectrum. The authors draw from their years of experience and vast knowledge to show that their Startup Corporation model is the way to deal with the innovation paradox."

   —Laizer Kornwasser, Company Group Chairman, Valeant Pharmaceuticals

"Many organizations are structurally committed to the status quo. Davila and Epstein offer practical ideas to overcome this challenge while preserving existing success."

   —Srikant Datar, Arthur Lowes Dickinson Professor, Harvard Business School

"In boardrooms, one of the most critical discussions centers around innovation and how to leverage creativity in the marketplace—faster and better than in the past. *The Innovation Paradox* demonstrates how to overcome obstacles and create breakthrough innovation."

   —Blythe McGarvie, member of the board of directors of Accenture, Viacom, LKQ
   Corporation, and Sonoco

The
Innovation
Paradox

WHY GOOD BUSINESSES
KILL BREAKTHROUGHS AND
HOW THEY CAN CHANGE

The
Innovation
Paradox

Tony Davila
Marc J. Epstein

BK

Berrett–Koehler Publishers, Inc.
San Francisco
a BK Business book

Berrett-Koehler Publishers, Inc.
235 Montgomery Street, Suite 650
San Francisco, CA 94104-2916
Tel: (415) 288-0260   Fax: (415) 362-2512   www.bkconnection.com

Ordering Information

Quantity sales. Special discounts are available on quantity purchases by corporations, associations, and others. For details, contact the "Special Sales Department" at the Berrett-Koehler address above.

Individual sales. Berrett-Koehler publications are available through most bookstores. They can also be ordered directly from Berrett-Koehler: Tel: (800) 929-2929; Fax: (802) 864-7626; www.bkconnection.com

Orders for college textbook/course adoption use. Please contact Berrett-Koehler: Tel: (800) 929-2929; Fax: (802) 864-7626.

Orders by U.S. trade bookstores and wholesalers. Please contact Ingram Publisher Services, Tel: (800) 509-4887; Fax: (800) 838-1149; E-mail: customer.service@ingrampublisherservices .com; or visit www.ingrampublisherservices.com/Ordering for details about electronic ordering.

Berrett-Koehler and the BK logo are registered trademarks of Berrett-Koehler Publishers, Inc.

Printed in the United States of America

Berrett-Koehler books are printed on long-lasting acid-free paper. When it is available, we choose paper that has been manufactured by environmentally responsible processes. These may include using trees grown in sustainable forests, incorporating recycled paper, minimizing chlorine in bleaching, or recycling the energy produced at the paper mill.

Cover design by Ian B. Koviak/The Book Designers

PRODUCED BY WILSTED & TAYLOR PUBLISHING SERVICES
Copyediting Melody Lacina   Design Nancy Koerner   Index Andrew Joron

Library of Congress Cataloging-in-Publication Data
Davila, Tony.
   The innovation paradox : why good businesses kill breakthroughs and how they can change / Tony Davila, Marc J. Epstein.
      pages cm
   Summary: "From the bestselling authors of *Making Innovation Work* (30,000 copies sold and translated into ten languages) comes a book that questions everything about how organizations innovate. Key takeaway: classical business management and corporate structures by their very nature will kill, not create, breakthroughs. The authors describe a new kind of organization—the startup corporation—that will make established companies as innovative as startups"—Provided by publisher.
   ISBN 978-1-60994-553-4 (hardback)
   1. Organizational change. 2. Technological innovations—Management. I. Epstein, Marc J. II. Title.
   HD58.8.D3698 2014
   658.4'063—dc23   2014012548

First edition

18 17 16 15 14   10 9 8 7 6 5 4 3 2 1

Contents

PREFACE

For most of the twentieth century, innovation was the territory of large organizations. Schumpeter argued that innovation should naturally happen within them. Innovation required significant amounts of resources—amounts that only large organizations had. Commencing in the 1960s with the first venture capital efforts,[1] the wall between smaller organizations—particularly startup companies coming out of universities—and innovation began to come down. The idea that scientific progress could hit the market through newly formed companies with venture funding rather than partnerships with established companies started to take hold. A different channel for breakthrough innovation—innovations with the potential to change industries and/or invent new ones—was created.

The growth of the Internet as a new field for social and business interactions in the 1990s fueled this channel for breakthrough innovation. By the time early online opportunities emerged, the venture capital model had been perfected and was ready to fund breakthrough innovation. The combination of a new funding vehicle and the Internet gave the competitive advantage to fast-moving startups. Leveraging a technology that changed how people relate to each other, these companies took advantage of business opportunities that opened up in almost every industry.

For nearly twenty years, high-growth startups have had much of the limelight when it comes to breakthrough innovation, dwarfing the efforts of established companies, which are seen as slow and unable to catch up. Yet large companies dominate most markets today, and their share grows. Their ability to execute has become their recipe for success—winners simply execute better.[2] Their operations are managed more efficiently, and a constant flux of incremental innovations—small, regular improvements to products and processes—keeps them in the lead. The business unit structure, invented a hundred years ago, has proven itself to be an effective organizational design—especially when it comes to scale and operational efficiency.

More importantly, the complexity of the business world and society at large means that innovative solutions are increasingly complex. Core ideas might be simple, but deploying effective business models requires access to resources, knowledge, networks, and execution power. Few innovations are successful as stand-alone propositions. Rather, they demand an ecosystem of complementary products, technologies, and services to be built around them.[3] For example, Better Place struggled when it attempted to build an infrastructure for electric cars. Energy is an intricate interface of production, transportation, and retailing that is hard to break, and changing the structure of an industry requires access to an entire network that will force it. Such access is often only available to large companies. Organizations that can mobilize many actors to implement solutions that address the challenges we face as a society are best suited to handle the level of complexity involved in innovation going forward.

This is not to say that startups will not contribute to innovation. On the contrary, they are best suited to develop a particular set of breakthrough innovations. Much like the typical corporate R&D lab approach popular in the mid-twentieth century, startups will survive, and will likely still be best equipped to develop breakthrough innovations focused on specific markets. Even the once dominant lone-inventor model—superseded and made largely obsolete by big labs—continues to exist and is successful in certain niches.[4]

A MYTH IN NEED OF DEBUNKING

The fact that many large organizations focus on incremental innovation—to reduce costs by an extra cent out of every unit and capture an extra inch of market with improved products and operations—has grown together with a myth: established companies cannot come up with the kind of breakthrough innovations that upset existing markets, create new industries, and generate extensive growth. The same myth ascribes the unique ability to develop breakthrough innovation to startup companies. Breakthrough innovation is the Achilles heel of large companies, the argument goes, and the statement is apt for quite a number of them.[5]

The benefits of pursuing operational excellence and incremental innovation can be liabilities for breakthrough innovation. Efforts to execute better often have the unintended consequence of reducing the likelihood of breakthrough innovation. In other words, the same organizational design that is good for improving operational excellence and developing incremental innovation can get in the way of breakthrough innovations that many leaders want. This, in a few words, is the innovation paradox.

It is hard to argue against efficiency, supply chain optimization, zero defects, and lower costs. As long as industry structures remain stable, a strategy focused on execution and incremental innovation is difficult to beat. But when new entrants or even aggressive incumbents redefine industries with breakthrough innovation, these execution-focused strategies are frequently deadly. The let's-hope-my-industry-stays-the-same "strategy" adhered to by certain companies is blind to the threat of someone else starting a whole new game of chess while they perfect their game of checkers.

As companies pursue breakthrough innovation, they typically invest larger and larger amounts of resources into the same places that have given them incremental innovation—the type of innovation they understand. In the process, what companies seldom realize is that they are more often than not limiting their own ability to develop breakthrough innovation. When breakthrough ideas are managed as incremental, they become incremental.

This book is about the paradox that arises when investments that are supposed to make companies more innovative actually end up making them less able to get the breakthroughs they are after. It is about operational excellence and incremental innovation as both sources of competitive advantage and seeds of breakthrough innovation failure. It is about recognizing that the organizational structures best adapted to efficiently execute a strategy based on the current environment can, at the same time, block the kind of transformation that comes with radical changes in the environment. The innovation paradox explains why managers feel the need to drastically change how innovation is managed, but can't seem to break away from the demands of incremental changes. It is also about defying this paradox.

DEFYING THE INNOVATION PARADOX

It seems counterintuitive. The same organizational structure, systems, culture, and practices that make some companies great on many dimensions can at the same time be the ones that limit their continued success. Shouldn't the best-equipped organizations also be able to compete effectively in creating growth? If the answer to this question is yes, then why is it often so hard? In most cases, the problem is not a lack of ideas or inspiration; it is a flawed design of how innovation is managed.

Many leaders have successfully designed their companies for better execution through improved performance management and accountability. In doing so, they better control their costs, and they incrementally improve their processes and products— but they seldom get the type of significant, breakthrough growth that disrupts current markets and creates new ones.

Yet various companies succeed in defying the innovation paradox. IBM reinvented itself after facing a near certain death. Apple revolutionized the mobile device market after having been dismissed as a relic of the past. Nespresso created a totally new market—coffee by the cup—now worth several billion dollars as part of the food giant Nestlé. 3M has consistently developed new markets since its birth more than one hundred years ago. These companies are merely the most visible part of an iceberg of established companies that succeed at bringing breakthrough innovations to the market. They prove that it can be done.

Louis Pasteur said that luck favors the prepared mind, and Picasso believed inspiration existed, but it had to find you working. Breakthroughs need both luck and inspiration, but companies designed to facilitate them are more likely to be successful than those just betting on luck and persistence. Chapter 1 explores the different faces of innovation and how each requires a distinct management approach.[6] The management structure for developing incremental innovation by setting demanding targets is very different from the structure that facilitates strategic discoveries— breakthrough innovation that emerges from the bottom of the organization. The concept of the Startup Corporation provides a way to design and operate organizations so that innovation is fostered at all levels, and managed effectively when breakthroughs occur. It is based on the belief that people with breakthrough ideas are found not only at the top but throughout the company, as well as in employees' outside networks. Not every company is like Apple under Steve Jobs, a leader who envisioned breakthroughs. Most established businesses have many visionaries within their fields and networks. The challenge is to bring these visionaries together to create a breakthrough.

Breakthroughs take time to mature, and they bring with them an uncertainty that companies largely focused on operational excellence often are not used to managing. Their return on investment (ROI) is harder to visualize, and many times no past model on which to base predictions exists. Breakthrough innovation includes deep collaboration and partnerships with outsiders such as universities, suppliers, future customers, and anybody with experience and expertise in the field. Its management balances access to a rich network and to the capabilities of the organization to execute. Chapter 2 explores the strengths of the business unit in promoting incremental innovation and its challenges to embrace breakthrough innovation efforts.

The Startup Corporation model identifies the fundamental traits of successful startup companies that large organizations must replicate to create both the space and the support for fostering breakthrough innovation. The model combines different organizational solutions to manage the breakthrough innovation process. Chapter 3 describes how startup companies manage innovation, and chapter 4 translates these ideas to established companies.

Companies use many tools to manage breakthrough innovation, and while some tools are designed to work best for certain stages of the innovation process, they do not necessarily reinforce others. Real solutions often encompass the combination of various tools and structures. Chapter 5 describes these different tools, while chapter 6 looks at ways to integrate them to effectively build a successful breakthrough innovation effort.

Breakthrough efforts are part of existing organizations that also work to deliver value from their current strategies. Embracing these two types of innovation requires an organization with a unique culture. Culture shapes people's reactions to issues as diverse as relying on outsiders for ideas, learning from (rather than punishing) failures, taking calculated risks, and going after hard but rewarding challenges. To foster innovation, culture must provide innovators with the resources necessary for developing ideas and supporting discovery. Chapter 7 discusses ways to foster innovative cultures.

Leaders of innovative organizations trust their people more than many would consider reasonable. They trust them to take calculated risks for learning fast and cheaply; to combine internal and external talent; and to accept failure. Chapter 8 deals with leadership for breakthrough innovation. Chapter 9 examines strategy, incentives, and management systems that provide the foundations for breakthrough innovation. Chapter 10 offers a few parting words to keep in mind.

WHY THIS BOOK?

The Innovation Paradox is the result of our constant attention to and interest in the management of innovation. It builds on the ideas of the 2006 book that we wrote together with one of the most knowledgeable people in this field, Robert Shelton. *Making Innovation Work: How to Manage It, Measure It, and Profit from It* has been translated into many languages, and a revised edition was recently released (2013). That book focused on implementing innovation strategies, and the root of its success was its presentation of innovation as a process that needs to be managed. Innovation is unique in several aspects—such as the relevance of creativity and the role of luck—but it still needs structure. *Making Innovation Work* provided frameworks and concepts to think about innovation strategies, cultures, measurement and incentives, and process design. It gave the infrastructure that translates creativity into value.

Though readers find that book helpful in developing processes for improving incremental innovation, they tell us that they continue to fail at implementing breakthroughs. These leaders, focused largely on execution and incremental innovation, want to know how they can spark breakthrough innovations that result in dramatic growth. Do they need to hire a creative genius who can see the future to lead the company? Why does it seem so easy for startups to develop products and services capable of causing major shifts in the market, while established companies often seem to find it impossible? Is it the people? the organizational structure? the systems? the culture? Is it a combination of all of these factors? The book in your hands addresses these questions.

We have spent a large part of our careers working with companies on the management of innovation. Our perspective has always been that cultures, leadership styles, structures, systems, and processes are what make things happen in organizations. This book is the result of our work and builds on previous academic and managerial concepts about breakthrough innovation. Many colleagues have provided valuable concepts and documented remarkable practices to help us better understand the many types and facets of innovation. These managers are leaders of organizations large and small, global and local, high-tech and low-tech, with R&D budgets big and little, and their companies often top the lists of innovative organizations. We have been privileged to work closely with these leaders and thank them for their significant support.

Though the two of us are located on separate continents and have worked in different industries, our experiences have been complementary. We have navigated distinct streams of working with managers, as well as researching and speaking with academic and managerial audiences. We have known each other for two decades, and our professional lives have crossed many times. We have co-written articles and co-edited books together, and have run conferences and consulting projects together. This book reflects not only the common themes in our professional lives, but also the pleasure of working with people that you respect, learn from, and—perhaps most important—enjoy.

To complete this project, we have relied on the experiences of hundreds of managers and academic leaders. Though we are unable here to thank each of them individually, we are grateful for their willingness to share both successes and failures. In addition, numerous colleagues have shared their knowledge, providing us with inspiration and guidance. Robert Shelton, our co-author in *Making Innovation Work*, has been a source of good discussions, great ideas, and constant encouragement. Jean-François Manzoni contributed immensely with helpful insights on innovation, especially concerning leadership and culture. We also want to thank the people who have supported the elaboration of this book. Pilar Parmigiani has generously shared her ideas. Nicolas Albert is a superb developmental editor, and our book is much improved due to his excellent work. Neal Maillet, our editor, and the entire team at Berrett-Koehler Publishers have been very helpful and a pleasure to work with.

We dedicate this book to our families, who always support us in our crazy lives as we attempt to better understand our societies and to add our small contribution to making the world a better place. The more you see established companies, nonprofit organizations, and startups, the more you appreciate their importance in coordinating the contributions of millions of people. Their managers are a crucial link to the well-being of our society. We also dedicate this book to them and their efforts to improve the practice of management.

1.

What Is the
Innovation Paradox?

NOKIA WAS A FINE-TUNED MACHINE when it came to grabbing the latest trends in mobile phone use and translating them
into robust, profitable designs. Its scouters mixed up with young
urban trendsetters, executives, and families, almost to the point
where they understood their customers better than they understood themselves. Techniques ranging from in-depth ethnogra-
phies to early prototyping helped the company keep its healthy
lead in mobile communication. For instance, the discovery that
people in countries such as Morocco and Ghana would share
phone conversations led Nokia to develop phones with more
powerful speakers, making it easier for more people to participate
in conversations.[1] Incremental innovations—gradual, regular improvements to existing products and services—allowed Nokia to
maintain and extend their lead in the market as they knew it.
What could possibly go wrong?

Nokia's market lead fell apart when the smart phone became
the mobile device of choice. Since the company was so successful in the market for traditional mobile phones, when the
market shifted away from their flagship products, Nokia was left
with a nearly perfect organization innovating for a market whose

relevance quickly eroded. Not only did Nokia lose its venerable market position, but it also lost any meaningful chance of making a dent in the smart phone market, allowing companies like Apple and Samsung to establish themselves.

Another example of creative destruction caused by break-through innovation—the kind of innovation that disrupts old markets and creates new ones—in the mobile communication industry is the ups and downs experienced by RIM (Research in Motion), the company behind the Blackberry. Blackberry was one of the early winners of the smart phone revolution, with a 22 percent market share in 2009. Executives praised its design and its security. *Businessweek* ranked it as the eighth most innovative company in the world. But by 2013, users were leaving Black-berry for new devices with more appealing features, and RIM's market share whittled down to 2.7 percent.[2] RIM kept executing on a strategy that had proven to be very successful, but one that had become obsolete in the fast-changing market.

The innovation paradox occurs when the aggressive pursuit of operational excellence and incremental innovation crowds out the possibility of creating breakthrough innovations. Its opposite is also often true—companies with a focus on developing break-throughs can lose their starting-line position to companies that simply execute better. What happened to Nokia with the advent of the smart phone, and RIM with the growing popularity of touch screens and other smart phone features, are merely two of many examples of companies that have fallen victim to the in-novation paradox.

Operational excellence and incremental innovation feed suc-cess within existing business models, but they can feed failure when it comes to creating new ones. The financial performance of incumbents frequently deteriorates quickly after an industry goes through a structural change. As Nokia and RIM discovered, by the time the structural change erodes the financial perfor-mance of incumbents, it is often too late for the leaders of the old market to catch up. Incremental innovation delivers results as long as the industry structure remains stable, yet it can fail miserably when breakthroughs redefine an industry.

Disruptive technologies and innovations cause drastic market changes.[3] The interesting thing is that incumbents often see them coming but then disregard them, to focus on incremental innovation. Nokia, for example, actually had a prototype of a smart phone. Yet their existing customers—the ones the company already knew and understood—were not asking for it. But if you simply ask people what they want, oftentimes the answer will be more of the same; consumers will often extrapolate from whatever is available today. Nokia was extremely successful with the phones they were selling, so why should they introduce a product their customers didn't even know they wanted? Hence, Nokia kept making improvements on models their customers liked. All the while a new market was about to form, taking with it many of those customers.[4]

Established companies can choose to disrupt markets through breakthrough innovation, or they can wait and hope: hope that their industries will not radically change, and that incremental innovation will keep on driving success. They can hope that the change will not be too abrupt and that they will be able to catch up; they can hope the change will only be a passing fad; they can lobby to stop the change; or they can be out in front and create the change.[5]

Operational excellence and incremental innovation succeed as long as an industry follows the predicted path. All industries experience breakthrough changes that make existing strategies obsolete. At these points, what made companies great can become their largest liability.

INCREMENTAL AND BREAKTHROUGH INNOVATION

Innovation is often mistakenly seen as a singular concept. Either your company is innovative, or it is not; either it's in your culture, or it's not. But innovation can best be understood as a range of types and intensities. At the ends of the spectrum are two markedly different phenomena—incremental innovation and breakthrough innovation (figure 1.1). Both have the goal of moving creativity to market, but similarities end soon after that.

Innovation is not a single concept. Failing to capture the differences in types of innovation throughout the management process leads to problems and frustrations.

Incremental innovation is about improvements, while breakthrough innovation is about discovery. Managers looking for the single best way to handle innovation are set to fail. As they search for the golden solution, they become frustrated when their innovation model fails to deliver the expected results. They conclude that their company does not have the culture and resources to achieve the feats they see in other organizations.

Incremental and breakthrough innovation (and all the shades in between) can be visualized as coming from a range of tech-

SPECTRUM OF INNOVATION

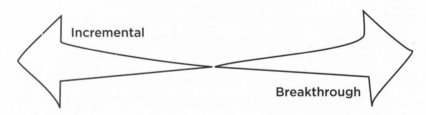

Incremental

Breakthrough

Figure 1.1. Types of innovation

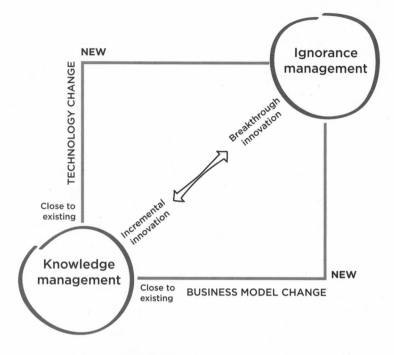

Figure 1.2. The innovation matrix[6]

nology and business models, some existing and others yet to be imagined (see figure 1.2).[7] Innovation works best when technological and business model dimensions are brought together. For example, the leadership of fashion firms often pair a creative mind—to come up with concepts that people had never considered—with a business mind—to bring those concepts to the market. Desigual, a fast-growing fashion firm, joined the creativity of Thomas Meyer with the business acumen of Manel Adell. Legendary design firms such as Christian Dior, Ralph Lauren, Prada, and Gucci also combine the separate talents of designers and businesspeople.[8]

Managing incremental innovation is about managing knowledge. Incremental innovation moves the current strategy forward. For instance, when Honda designs its new Odyssey, it isn't reinventing the automobile. Instead, a new version of an older model likely includes a nice set of novelties. Its safety features are better, its technology makes driving easier, and its entertainment capabilities are enhanced, but most of the parameters that define the car are unchanged.

In contrast, managing breakthrough innovation is about managing ignorance and uncertainties. For instance, consider the questions surrounding the driverless car: Which technology works best? How will people use it? How will it be commercialized? Will it coexist with or replace traditional cars? Will we need garages? How will traffic be regulated on driverless roads? As innovation efforts move away from existing products and services toward new technologies and new business models, uncertainty increases, risk goes up, and knowledge is sparser.

B reakthrough innovation deals with much higher levels of uncertainty and risk, and lower levels of knowledge. Thus, it needs to be managed differently from incremental innovation.

The two extremes of innovation are so different that they can't be managed the same way, and how you manage determines what you get.[9] If what begins as breakthrough innovation is managed as incremental, more likely than not it will become an incremental innovation. Sure, luck plays a substantial role, and a company may be lucky and get a breakthrough from an incremental innovation process. But putting more and more money into traditional incremental innovation processes will probably not significantly increase the already small odds of getting a breakthrough. Table 1.1 describes the main differences between incremental and breakthrough innovation.

Incremental Innovation

Most companies are good at developing innovations that build upon and advance the current strategy—innovations that fit within existing technologies and business models. Such developments help create operational excellence. A large percentage of investments go to feed this sort of innovation, the kind that keeps an organization in the game and gives it an edge over competitors. It is a hugely important type of innovation. Moreover, little steps, if they are taken faster than the pace of competitors, can put a company in the leadership position.

Winning in established markets requires executing faster through incremental innovation cycles. Even in maturing markets, the end-winner is the company able to better execute. Fast seconds—companies that come from behind to dominate markets—often end up at the top of the game.[10] Apple largely created the market for smart phones and tablets through the iPhone-iPad revolution, but Google and Samsung have been claiming territory with relentless efforts to bring incremental concepts to market. Pioneers such as Sixdegrees and MySpace explored social media early on, only to see Facebook take the lion's share of the market, LinkedIn succeed in professional networks, and Twitter take the short communication space.

Table 1.1. Comparing incremental and breakthrough innovation

BREAKTHROUGH INNOVATION	INCREMENTAL INNOVATION
Talent combined for discovery and execution	Talent with strong weight on execution
Funding from separate budget	Funding from business units
Staged funding	Funding based on budgets
Low chance of success	Larger chance of success
Large returns on investment	Lower returns on investment
Discovery driven	Execution driven
Qualitative assessment	Financial metrics

Incremental innovation operates with relatively low amounts of uncertainty, large amounts of knowledge, and often large amounts of resources as well. It benefits from structured processes, because processes are good at managing knowledge and resources efficiently. For example, Logitech has dominated the computer peripheral market for more than a decade now. Every year, they come up with mice, keyboards, and web cams that are better than earlier versions. When Logitech goes into designing these new products, it already knows what the majority of these products will look like. It knows when the new products have to be on the market, the technologies that will go into them, their price points, their features, and a quite accurate development budget estimate. Of course, some uncertainties exist—like whether the new design will appeal to the consumer, or the new features will be better than those of competitors. But these uncertainties pale in comparison to the uncertainties of building industries around "not-yet" markets, like space tourism, nano-robots, or an ageless society.

Incremental innovation is extremely important for sustaining competitive advantage in current markets, and its inspiration benefits mostly from in-depth customer knowledge. Back in early 2000, Logitech, the leader in computer peripherals, had no presence in the keyboard market. One of its marketing department studies asked consumers to name the most important keyboard manufacturers, and even though Logitech had never made a keyboard, it came out as number three on the survey. A lot of companies would discard this information, or discount it as showing how ignorant consumers are—after all, Logitech knew that it had never sold a keyboard. Instead, the company interpreted it as a clear message to get into the market. In the minds of consumers, Logitech built and designed great mice, so they should also make great keyboards. Since keyboards use existing technology and were manufactured and distributed through the same channels as mice, Logitech's innovation was far from breakthrough. Yet it became a large and profitable business, and Logitech eventually ended up grabbing the number-one position.

Incremental innovation also benefits from going beyond customer needs into customer motivations. Design thinking and human-centered design effectively use careful observation and patient efforts to determine what people need and why people behave the way they do. They help understand that products not only fulfill a function but also have social and emotional meanings.

Incremental innovation operates with relatively low levels of uncertainty, benefits from established processes, and is extremely important for sustaining competitive advantage in current markets.

Overall, incremental innovation is a fundamental aspect of winning—it can result in rapid improvements for customers as well as for the organization, and it can keep company morale up by maintaining momentum. In fact, incremental innovation is central for staying competitive in current markets, and for defending new developments. While incremental innovation has barriers to achievement, the other end of the spectrum of intensity—breakthrough innovation—is a whole different beast altogether.

Breakthrough Innovation

In 1926, Henry Ford designed an airplane for the mass market—his idea being that everybody would fly an airplane much like they drove a car. The idea of personal planes is still appealing, and various research groups today are working to make this idea a reality. Should these groups successfully design the product and the business model to make it available to a large number of consumers, a lot of the infrastructure that we take for granted will be questioned, and additional infrastructure will need to be created. A world in which individuals pilot planes with the regularity that people now drive cars would certainly be a new paradigm, and would require a whole slew of support systems and structures.

Breakthrough innovations redefine paradigms and offer new ways to look at the world. Breakthroughs are often swift and spectacular, but they can also evolve over longer periods of time.

Breakthrough innovation can shift existing paradigms. It is much riskier than incremental innovation, and the quest for it often fails, but it holds huge potential for growth. When breakthrough innovation succeeds, it creates new markets and redefines industries; incumbents often lose their dominant positions in favor of the mavericks who took the risk to change their industries and won. Its effects can be devastating to companies that failed to gauge its implications on their customer base, and it can truly disrupt the status quo.

The most visible breakthrough innovations act quickly and revolutionize industries in very short periods of time. Often they create and leverage new technologies that rapidly make existing ones obsolete. For example, the iPod and the business model around it all but banished other portable music devices, while smart phones put companies focused on more traditional mobile devices in a difficult position. By the time the performance of disruptive technologies catches up with the incumbents' technologies, the incumbents are often hard pressed to develop a way to compete in the new market.

In other cases, breakthrough innovations are crafted over several years and take longer to fully transform industries. The international fashion company Zara is an example. In a market traditionally dependent on seasons and advertising in traditional media, trial and error in Zara's early years helped them shape a robust, disruptive, and winning business model. Whereas fashion was once an almost exclusively seasonal event, it is now a constant flow. Design cycles are measured in weeks rather than months; products that are sold out are not replenished; and print advertising is not needed to bring people into the shop. Zara has challenged deeply ingrained assumptions about how people shop for clothes, and how companies should serve them—and it has paid off. Breakthrough innovation is about questioning our values and beliefs, our mental models of how industries work, and our assumptions.

Breakthrough innovation is not only about managing uncertainty and learning from successes; it is also about learning from failures. The CEO of an innovative engineering company with stellar performance at one time argued, "if we want to grow beyond our existing business model, we need to learn to defend the solutions that we conquered. We are very good at attacking, but we are not able to defend our positions." The company was set up for groundbreaking innovations, but the company failed to manage the incremental steps necessary to maintain a position once it had taken it. Breakthrough innovation needs to be followed by a constant flow of high-quality incremental innovation. It is great to break new ground, but the value of your innovation can quickly slip away to competitors if you can't defend it.

A lot of the frustration surrounding innovation efforts in companies is the result of hoping to get breakthrough ideas

---

Incremental innovation is about employing creativity within existing strategies and industry structures. Breakthrough innovation is about employing creativity to come up with new strategies, new industries, and new societies.

---

when structures and processes are largely set up for incremental innovation.

The last decade has seen different emphases on open and closed innovation. Some companies still believe in a closed model, but most organizations have embraced a more open model, in which internal resources and external networks are combined to optimize the innovation process. Open models are even more important for breakthrough innovations. For example, the model used in university research has always emphasized collaboration and the open exchange of ideas. Breakthrough innovations coming out of universities are the culmination of lots of small steps from different research groups across the globe. An old adage says, "Visionaries see more because they stand on the shoulders of giants," and open access to knowledge builds these giants. In that same spirit, companies like IBM, Nokia, and Sony have made their patents related to improving the environment available for free on the Eco-Patent Commons platform. People can use this intellectual property to come up with environmentally friendly innovations. Other initiatives, such as Green Xchange, intend to create communities for people to exchange ideas, knowledge, and patents concerning environmental innovations.[11] But the idea of open innovation isn't only about giving things away, or making things freely available—it's also about creating networks that work together to address bigger opportunities.

TOP-DOWN AND BOTTOM-UP INNOVATION

Another difference in the features of incremental and breakthrough innovation is the tension between top-down and bottom-up innovation. If you want breakthrough innovation but manage it as incremental, odds are a big breakthrough won't happen. Similarly, if you want bottom-up innovation but the company is managed using a top-down approach, people will not contribute. Managers are often surprised that their employees fail to come up with ideas. What they don't realize is that their day-to-day message is for people to execute ideas originating at the top. Xerox's PARC research center has become a classic illustration of headquarters missing out on opportunities to capitalize on ideas generated at the bottom of the organization. The company set up the right environment—smart people in a stimulating environment with resources to explore radical ideas. Yet it failed to channel those ideas into new Xerox businesses. In fact, the ideas ended up creating significant value outside Xerox.

Innovation coming from the top requires a different management approach than bottom-up innovation. The latter requires not only having a rich environment but also having mechanisms for nurturing and moving ideas within the organization.

Managing innovation top-down is a different process than if innovation bubbles up from the bottom of the organization and its networks. The Apple-Google contrast illustrates this distinction. Apple's success was largely dependent on the genius of Steve Jobs, who had the vision and courage to take risks and to steer the company into unexplored products and markets. Apple was designed to implement this top-down vision. A functional structure implemented the ideas coming from top management. The full perspective on new ventures was limited to a handful of people; different sections of the company worked on pieces of these ventures without necessarily understanding the whole. The success of this approach to breakthrough innovation hinges on the visionary leader being right about the radically different future. Of course, the vision gets embedded into the company culture, and Apple's culture reflected Jobs's passion for products ahead of financial performance. Actually, financials were a result of the obsession for great products.[12]

Google's breakthrough innovation model, on the other hand, is grounded on letting ideas bubble up. The company encourages employees to toy with new ideas and then gambles on those that appear to be the most promising. It relies on letting inspiration flow from the organization.[13] The company bets on attracting the best talent and follows up by giving them the freedom and resources necessary to explore and flourish. Jeff Bezos, Amazon.com's founder and CEO, has referred to the importance of urging people throughout the company to innovate: "I encourage our employees to go down blind alleys and experiment. If we can get processes decentralized so that we can do a lot of experiments without it being very costly, we'll get a lot more innovation."[14]

A bottom-up model of innovation is hardly compatible with a company in which top management sees the organization as a vehicle to implement its vision, and a company with a strong top-down orientation is unlikely to get breakthrough ideas rising from the bottom. The kind of innovation your organization develops has much to do with how your organization is oriented and managed.

MANAGING FOR STRATEGIC DISCOVERIES

A global company in the data management industry designed a tournament challenging employees to identify new growth platforms beyond existing businesses. The objective was to tap into the collective creativity of employees around the world to generate breakthrough innovations. The tournament was set up so that early rounds happened within established business units. Each business unit then selected the projects that made it to the final round at headquarters.

The resulting ideas were great, and top management was more than happy to provide further funding to most of them. But they still weren't really what management was looking for. Each and every idea that employees came up with over the course of the tournament was incremental. Each built on the existing strategy of the business unit, targeted the same customers, and fit squarely into how the structure of the industry was perceived at the company. There was not a radical disruption in the bunch, and top management lost most of its faith in the possibility of first-rate ideas originating with employees.

But the outcome was fully predictable. The way the tournament was structured—forming teams within business units, and having business units be the first judges—reinforced the kind of incremental innovation that this established organization had grown to master. Not surprisingly, when the business units chose the best ideas, each one championed concepts that reinforced their existing strategies—the sort of incremental innovation that best supports execution.

Managing as if there were only one single model of innovation is in a way self-fulfilling—it tends to lead to a single kind of innovation. The phrase "How you innovate determines what you innovate" encapsulates this idea.[15] The innovation processes an organization has in place will shape what that organization can do, and the intersections of innovation types and management approaches lead to four distinct models for managing innovation, as summarized in figure 1.3.[16]

Existing concepts in innovation management provide a limited perspective on these four innovation models. The exploration-exploitation dichotomy does a great job of describing the

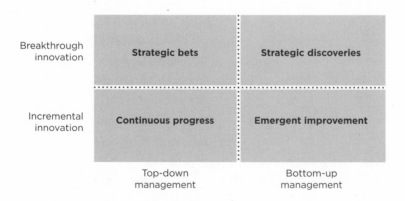

Top-down
management

Bottom-up
management

Figure 1.3. Management models for innovation

incremental-radical dimension. Exploration is about discovering, while exploitation is about utilizing incremental ideas to move businesses forward. Exploitation can either be pushed top-down through demanding targets that force people to move their business model forward, or be opened to bottom-up contributions that stimulate and develop ideas. Exploration can pursue radical ideas from top management or encourage the ingenuity of people throughout the company. The concept of ambidextrous organizations highlights the need for large, established players to combine incremental and breakthrough innovation. It also reinforces the tension between managing incremental and breakthrough innovation: the incremental-radical paradox. But it does not reflect the top-down versus bottom-up paradox—the fact that organizations managed in a top-down manner will struggle to find innovative ideas percolating up from the bottom.

Continuous Progress

The type of innovation that many established organizations already excel at developing is *continuous progress*—innovation that improves on current technology and business models. A range of management tools has been designed over the last 150 years to deliver on top-down incremental innovation.

Continuous progress starts with top management setting more demanding objectives for each upcoming period. Top management often uses strategic planning to synthesize ideas into specific objectives for a designated time. These objectives incorporate improvement goals, investment decisions, and new management processes and structures. Difficult but achievable targets, opera-

---

Continuous progress—top-down incremental innovation— is paramount to gain and maintain competitive advantage in stable markets. Strategic planning and demanding targets force people to innovate to meet goals.

---

tional budgets, nonfinancial performance measures, and investment budgets are some of the tools used for continuous progress.[17] These objectives force people to work harder, as well as be creative in finding new ways to meet their goals. As long as the competitive landscape is stable without extreme changes that threaten the status quo, this type of innovation is paramount to success.

Emergent Improvements

Whereas continuous progress induces people to be creative to meet their goals, *emergent improvements* encourage people from the bottom up to be inventive. This model for innovation makes space for people to suggest incremental developments to current products and services. Creativity workshops, brainstorming sessions, idea competitions, storytelling, and idea tournaments are all efforts to leverage the creativity of people in the larger company. They challenge the idea that top managers are the only creative employees. Yet such bottom-up innovation activities require proper management tools and structures to avoid losing potentially valuable ideas.

Emergent improvements are the result of structured processes to stimulate and capture ideas from the bottom of the organization.

The customer is at the center of emergent improvements. In fact, the most important part of incremental product and service innovation is a thorough understanding of the customer. Having a feel for customers, processes, technologies, and industries helps organizations execute better than their competitors. Such understanding is easier to achieve in close contact; customer research techniques in which people "live" with customers—not unlike the way ethnographers do to better understand societies—are often the first steps. Emergent improvements also benefit from tapping networks outside the company and leveraging their ideas. Part of the challenge, then, is to motivate people, stimulate their curiosity, and give them a channel for bringing their ideas to decision makers.

Strategic Bets

Breakthrough innovation in established companies is often driven from top management choosing a risky but potentially high-return strategy to implement across an organization. Its success depends on both the insight of its creator's vision—whether the leader is betting on the right future scenario to play out—and a company's ability to execute on that vision. Apple with Steve Jobs at the helm exemplifies an organization capable of bringing a breakthrough innovation to market.

Strategic bets are leader-centric and execution driven.[18] The leaders who make them often have traits of genius. They are the Hitchcocks and Coppolas of business, so to speak: people who envision the future and work with many other creative people to make it happen. When successful, they transform companies, industries, and sometimes even society. However, the strategic bet innovation model hinges on the quality of a leader's vision and the ability of an organization to execute on it. If the leader's vision is off, the organization executes into a brick wall. Successful startups are built on the vision of their founders, yet their success or failure depends on whether they perform better than anybody else. Winners in the startup world are not necessarily the ones with the best ideas; they are the ones who are best at adapting and executing.

Strategic bets are breakthroughs that come from the top of an organization. They depend on people at the top having the right vision and an organization ready to execute on this vision.

Strategic bets are common for companies hit by a structural change in their industry. As companies see their financial performance sinking, they go after strategic bets as the life raft that might save them. While they can look appealing when a supposedly tried-and-true strategy starts to falter, strategic bets in turnaround situations add the urgency to perform to the uncertainty of breakthrough innovation. The outcome is often failure.

Strategic Discoveries

Not every organization has a visionary leader with a clear vision of the future, and no visionary leader is right every time. *Strategic discoveries*—the focus of this book—are breakthroughs that result from harnessing the insights of many people throughout an organization and its networks. Strategic discoveries are about combining the talent, inspiration, and vision of people with different expertise: the hidden geniuses. They bring together many visionaries to create a breakthrough masterpiece.

S trategic discoveries are breakthrough innovations that result from bringing together the genius of many people throughout an organization and its networks.

Strategic discoveries are about trusting the people in your organization rather than betting on the inspiration of a few at the top. Smart people, especially gifted ones within a field, are far more likely to be found among employees and their external networks as numbers grow. It is simply the law of large numbers—the chance of finding a person with talent and a wonderful idea is much greater in a group of 10,000 people than it is in a group of 20. This approach leverages not only the creativity within a company but also the creativity in its network. (For a comparison of approaches to innovation management, see table 1.2.)

Table 1.2. Comparing innovation management approaches

TYPE OF APPROACH	DESCRIPTION
Continuous progress	Top-down planning and incremental goal setting that induce people to innovate in their effort to meet those goals
Emergent improvements	Results from structured processes to stimulate and capture incremental ideas throughout the organization
Strategic bets	Attempts at breakthrough innovations that depend on a leader's vision and an organization's ability to execute
Strategic discoveries	Breakthrough innovations that result from harnessing the collective genius of the organization and its networks

Strategic discoveries require a unique combination of organizational skills. Leaders at the helm of the company must create a trusting culture in which people are willing to take risks, and to do so without fear of making mistakes. Employees also need to learn to cope with not knowing the destiny of the company (leaders are supposed to know where the company is going!). But when you trust your people and believe in their ability to discover new strategies and business models, you relinquish some control. While the CEO still ultimately directs the evolution of current strategy, she does not necessarily know where future radical growth opportunities will come from. The CEO is not the traditional captain who knows where the ship is going better than anybody else. She knows what the next port will be, but she lets the crew identify the following one. And she allows them to chart the currents as they are, not as she would like them to be. Her job then becomes more one of facilitating the process of discovery than of pointing out the way.

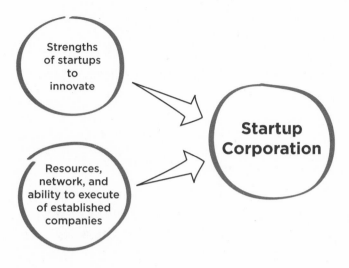

Figure 1.4. The Startup Corporation

THE STARTUP CORPORATION

Whether an organization has 30 or 30,000 employees, going after strategic discoveries—bottom-up breakthrough innovation—requires a management approach that brings together the diverse resources available to an established company and the ingenuity of startup companies. The Startup Corporation is a set of management tools inspired by the way startup ecosystems are designed for exploration that allows established organizations to leverage their resources. In other words, the Startup Corporation emphasizes the strengths of startups when it comes to developing breakthroughs, but spotlights the strengths of established organizations when it comes to scaling and execution (see figure 1.4).

The characteristics of the Startup Corporation give it certain distinct advantages in avoiding the pitfalls of the innovation paradox. First, whereas companies like Nokia and RIM have seen

---

The Startup Corporation provides the organizational tools to manage strategic discoveries—breakthrough innovations resulting from the combination of the insights of people throughout an organization and its networks.

---

their markets vanish with the advent of new ones, the Startup Corporation adapts management to the needs of breakthrough innovation. For instance, it devotes a portion of time, energy, and resources to exploring not-yet markets with the gusto of a startup, while still allowing the larger organization to focus on the incremental innovations that made and continue to make it a success.

On the opposite side of the coin, once the Startup Corporation begins to close in on a viable product or service, it can leverage the parent company's resources, networks, and ability to execute. Figure 1.5 illustrates the activities of strategic discoveries that established companies need to manage in utilizing the Startup Corporation. These activities are comparable to the ones startups engage in on the way from idea to market, but they also take into account the access to resources that is unique to established companies. (While we present these activities in sequence, they go back and forth and often happen simultaneously.)

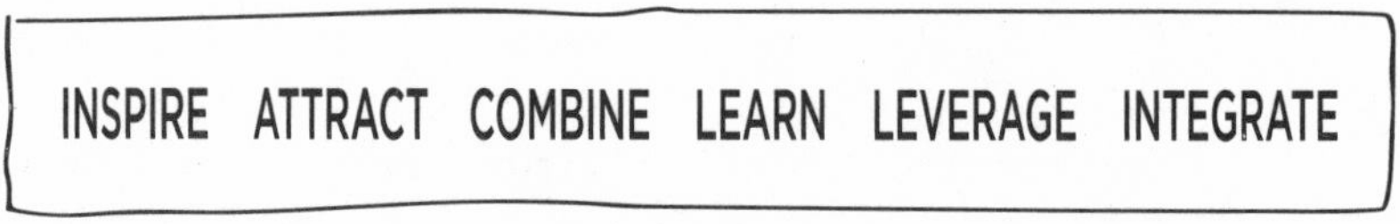

INSPIRE ATTRACT COMBINE LEARN LEVERAGE INTEGRATE

Figure 1.5. Managing strategic discoveries with the Startup Corporation

What good is it if you excel at inspiring people to have fresh ideas but fail to ultimately move those ideas to market in a meaningful way? Managing breakthrough innovation requires the Startup Corporation to handle each of the different activities of strategic discoveries: inspire, attract, combine, learn, leverage, and integrate.

The first activity—*inspire*—is about creating rich environments that stimulate people to come up with new ideas. Unlike top-down models that bet on the vision of a few, the Startup Corporation survives on the creative input of its members and their networks.

The Startup Corporation values the networks of all people in the organization. The *attract* activity highlights the openness that breakthrough innovation requires by fostering productive relationships among mutually beneficial partners. And though the lone tinkerer in a garage still yields the occasional breakthrough, some of the best are the result of a cross-pollination of organizations and industries. The *combine* activity reflects the complexity of breakthrough innovation by bringing together seemingly disparate ideas to create new solutions.

Breakthrough innovation is about experimenting. It is about determining what works and what doesn't, and uncovering which assumptions are right, and which are wrong. The *learn* activity revolves around processes of discovery and experimentation that are central to breakthrough innovation.

The inherent advantage a Startup Corporation has as part of a larger organization is its ability to *leverage* that organization's resources. Rather than needing to search for specific knowledge, networks, or support activities, the Startup Corporation has the backing (and resources) of its parent company. The final activity—*integrate*—is transitioning to the execution mentality that has made the larger organization successful, where operational excellence and incremental innovation will determine long-term success.

Since the Startup Corporation is situated within an established company, its success largely depends on how it is set up, as well as on the support it receives from the parent company. Without strong foundations (see figure 1.6), the most advanced efforts for breakthrough innovation stand a great chance of failing.

Even with all of the foundations in place, getting a breakthrough innovation to market in a meaningful way—and turning that breakthrough into anything more than a passing fad—requires the ability to execute and the ability to innovate incrementally.

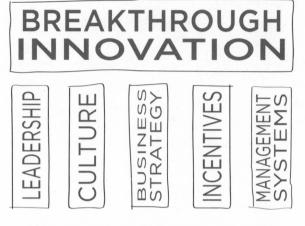

Figure 1.6. Designing for breakthrough innovation

THE TRUTH ABOUT THE INNOVATION PARADOX

After its big coffee-by-the-cup breakthrough, Nespresso has kept its premium position in the coffee market through a constant flow of incremental innovations to its products and its business model. Facebook built on top of previous breakthrough innovations to create the most successful social network. Yet Facebook's continued financial success depends on a steady stream of innovations—most of them incremental—to monetize the social interactions that happen through the network.

While a strong offense often revolves around breakthroughs, defense is about incremental innovation, and established companies know how to manage it. Companies need to be good at operational excellence and incremental innovation, because without them, survival is at stake. Every year, companies need to incrementally push the boundaries of today's technologies and business models; they must come up with new products, reduce their costs, improve their processes, know their customers better, and gain that incremental margin and growth that gives them a lead over competitors—or at least keeps them in the game.

In stable industries, companies that excel at incremental innovation accumulate a significant lead over competitors. For example, Toyota's rise to leadership in the car industry is grounded on its ability to follow up breakthroughs in managing manufacturing and hybrid technology with continual incremental innovations better than anybody else. Similarly, Southwest Airlines' success lies in consistently improving upon a business model that it invented more than thirty years ago. However, concentrating on the incremental also creates a number of challenges. If incremental innovation is considered the norm, ideas with breakthrough potential may become a rarity. When new ideas do surface, a narrow focus on enhancing current strategy can contribute to an organization's failure to capitalize on those opportunities. Companies simply get stuck in their old ways, while markets shift and form around them.

The innovation paradox is sticky, and an established organization or leader may be tempted to hold on to what is working and forgo the costly risks that can produce breakthrough innovations. But incremental innovation isn't and can't be everything. Markets can change drastically—and even disappear. The truth is, both incremental innovation and breakthrough innovation are immensely important in their own ways. For an organization to thrive in the long run, it needs to be able to capitalize on breakthrough innovations when they occur while continuing to innovate incrementally and build competitive advantage every day.

B reakthrough innovation, when successful, requires a constant stream of incremental innovation to maintain the original lead.

EXTERNAL NEED FOR INNOVATION

- What potential changes in the industry may make my organization's strategy obsolete?
- What is the potential impact of emerging trends on my organization's strategy?
- Can my organization lead big changes in the industry?
- Can my organization create new markets?
- Is my organization getting the right amount of innovation it needs for the short and long term?
- Is my organization leading or lagging behind competitors in incremental innovation?
- Is my organization leading or lagging behind competitors in breakthrough innovation?

INTERNAL PUSH FOR INNOVATION

- What have been my organization's ingredients for success?
- What is my organization doing to improve its innovation performance?
- What type of innovation does my organization support best?
- In my organization, what is leadership's position toward the various types of innovation?

MANAGEMENT OF INNOVATION

- How does my organization manage strategic discoveries?
- How does my organization manage strategic bets?
- How does my organization manage emergent improvements?
- How does my organization manage continuous progress?
- How can my organization improve these different processes?

The Benefits and Limits
of the Business Unit

BUSINESS UNITS date back to the 1930s, when General Motors took the leadership position in the car market from Ford.[1] Ford had become extremely good at process innovation during that decade—streamlining its operations to be the lowest-cost automobile producer—but General Motors was better at reading the consumer of the time. While Ford was busy working to keep costs down, GM was capturing new market segments for which price was not the main purchasing criterion. More than one car market existed, and GM restructured its organization to serve multiple markets. Contrary to the traditional functional organization, GM was divided into business units—each focused on a particular market segment, each with its own brand, each run as if it were an independent company (figure 2.1). This structure proved to be much faster than the traditional organization at capturing the demands of customers and translating them into new designs.

The widespread use of divisional structures and business units speaks to their success.[2] Razor focused on execution in a particular market, they beat any alternative management solution developed thus far. In the absence of industry revolutions, execution

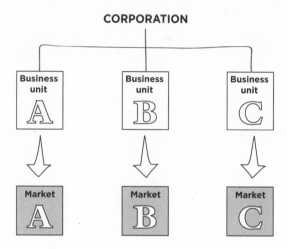

Figure 2.1. The business unit structure

and the ability to manage incremental innovation decide winners and losers. Focusing on being more efficient, more attentive to shifts in customer needs, and more creative in addressing and fulfilling customer needs pays off.

However, while it is hard to argue against smooth, efficient, and low-cost operations, the better a company becomes at executing its existing business model, the less attention it generally pays to the development of breakthrough innovations. Ford's early focus on continually improving cost savings is another illustration of the innovation paradox—the way relentless pursuit of incremental innovation often crowds out the possibility of breakthrough innovation. The temptation is for managers to favor ideas that reinforce the existing strategy rather than consider those that challenge it.

Responding to shifts in industries, some incumbents misguidedly double their current efforts, essentially doing more of what they are already doing. For example, before refrigerators existed, ice was used to keep things cold. The ice-harvesting industry constantly improved each of the various stages of the value chain: growing ice in lakes, harvesting ice, transporting ice, and storing ice. When the refrigerator was invented—a breakthrough innovation at the time—it seriously challenged this well-established industry. At first, the refrigerator was dismissed as an inferior technology—one that was much more expensive, and noisy. As consumers became receptive to the refrigerator and its performance proved to be a real threat, the ice-harvesting industry essentially put its blinders on. Ice providers did not shift their strategy to include the new technology that was eroding their business. Instead, they kept improving the efficiency of their existing processes. The most significant improvement in ice-harvesting technology actually happened when the refrigerator had already achieved dominance—long after the development would have made any difference.[3]

But the innovation paradox is tricky. Just because someone has a great idea does not necessarily mean that they will execute it best. Fast seconds—often the winners in new markets—do not come up with the original breakthrough idea, but they win because of their ability to copy, improve, and execute better. While breakthrough innovation can disrupt and create new markets, it can't do much of anything without execution.

Business units have proven to be very effective at stimulating incremental innovation. Their focus on specific market segments—products or geographies, technologies, and competitors—enables easier target setting, performance measurement, and course correction. In environments that are changing faster than ever before, however, new technologies can quickly alter the rules of the game. Industry boundaries become increasingly fluid, leading to the emergence of new competitors from environments

---

Business units are razor focused on execution, and incremental innovation is integral to staying ahead of competitors. Yet incremental innovation often crowds out breakthrough innovation in this organizational design.

---

that previously didn't exist, or that were traditionally off these business units' radar screen. Unless an organization makes a concerted effort to look beyond today's markets, technologies, and competitors, its focus on execution and incremental innovation can become a handicap when adapting to rapid and profound change.

THE BENEFITS OF BUSINESS UNITS

Business units are generally organized using a structure based on functions. Core functions reside at the business unit level, while support functions are often centralized to gain from economies of scale and scope. This structure is designed to deliver value through flawless execution and a good dose of incremental innovation. Like an Olympic swimmer who trains and trains to cut a hundredth of a second off her time, business units compete to get that extra point of market share or reduce costs by a percentage point. Table 2.1 lists some of the advantages of utilizing business units based on a functional structure.

Business Units Excel at Execution and Guiding Continuous Progress

Successful, established companies are superb at execution. Sure, many of them started with a breakthrough idea, but an idea in itself does not make a successful business over the long term. For

Table 2.1. Advantages of the business unit structure

Excels at execution and guiding continuous progress
Encourages incremental innovations that advance existing strategies through targeted resource allocation
Creates economic and social value with demanding cultures while balancing risk and motivation
Manages emergent improvements

example, Inditex, the company behind Zara and other clothing brands, came up with a radical approach to commercializing fashion, but its continued success depends on its ability to execute on and constantly improve upon its business model. Walmart's original idea to establish large stores in rural Midwestern cities gave the company its start, but keeping "everyday low prices" requires constant effort to improve operations.[4]

Business units, based on functional structures, are hard to beat as long as the industry structure remains stable. Yet their strength is diluted when facing structural changes in the industry.

Most markets tend to remain stable for long periods. Their structure varies slightly and slowly, and they seldom experience radical changes to their technologies or their business models. During these stretches of stability, perfecting execution is the best way to get the most value out of an existing business model. Like that same swimmer training for the Olympics, tracking progress also requires constant measurement. While capital markets focus on quarterly earnings, monitoring can be an ongoing activity within business units. The business unit itself can measure its financial performance monthly or weekly; it can keep tabs on nonfinancial performance measures daily, or even hourly. Since execution leaves little room for efforts that do not pay off within a reasonably short amount of time, quickly knowing what's working and what isn't allows business units to respond effectively.

Business Units Encourage Incremental Innovations through Targeted Resource Allocation

Another benefit of business units is their ability to encourage incremental innovations that advance existing strategies through

Table 2.2. Resource allocation for top-down incremental innovation

FOCUS	FUNCTION
Platform technologies	Advance the technologies of the existing business to make it more competitive
Product innovation	Develop manufactured and service products to offer customers a better proposal
Process improvements	Advance processes to enhance customer service and lower costs
Management improvements	Enhance management of the organization to better respond to market shifts
Market positioning	Merge and acquire competitors to consolidate markets

targeted resource allocation. The traditional approach to incremental innovation is driven from top management in a few ways, one of them being resource allocation. These decisions are then primarily evaluated in terms of financial returns. Of course, other criteria come into play, but it's hard to argue against financial returns. Investments with higher expected returns will have a higher priority.

The way top management allocates investments heavily affects how incremental innovation will play out. For example, a company that invests heavily in supply-chain software will open up more options to improve the management of its supply chain than will a company that invests strictly in improving the technology of its products. That said, management can allocate resources to a number of places as part of strategies for incremental innovation, and top management investment decisions—whether to invest more in a certain business unit than another—send important messages about current priorities (table 2.2).

Investing in platform technologies. Today's R&D investments focus on technologies that have a clear application in existing businesses. For instance, making a detergent with stronger cleaning power or a lower environmental impact requires a large investment. Few companies direct a significant portion of their R&D to breakthroughs, as Bell Labs did with the transistor in the 1950s. While some companies are able to transform happy accidents into new markets, the R&D labs' central purpose is to advance the mid- to long-term technology needs of existing businesses.

Investing in product innovation. Incremental innovation investments go into product development in the form of designs for new versions of existing products. Succeeding at product innovation requires intense customer intimacy, and well-managed business units are skilled at getting to know their customers.

Investing in process improvements. Innovation budgets also include investments in process improvements to increase efficiency and quality, reduce costs, and enhance customer satisfaction. Process innovation often is acquired through adopting new hardware and software from external suppliers.

Investing in management improvements. Investments to improve the management of the organization—making it more efficient and better at meeting customer needs—take the form of software, training, and consulting. All management processes now utilize software; training transfers knowledge in the organization so that employees can improve execution; and consulting allows for innovation to be acquired from external suppliers and adapted to the needs of the company.

The way top management allocates investments heavily affects how incremental innovation will play out. Continuous progress comes from top management's planning process and how its investment decisions advance existing strategies.

Investing to improve market positioning. Investments to improve market positioning are often associated with acquisitions that consolidate the industry and give the buyer a stronger bargaining position, or that offer an entry point to a new geography or market. The success and failure of acquisitions hinge on the ability to execute on the integration of the acquisition.

Business Units Create Value with Demanding Cultures while Balancing Risk and Motivation

Investments to reinforce incremental innovation are often sizeable, and deciding where to allocate resources is never a sure thing. Even if the uncertainty is low, the financial impact of investments that end up failing can be dangerously high. For instance, initial tests of a high-speed train track discovered that the ballast of the track was hitting the bottom of the train when train speeds were high. The unexpected effect ultimately limited the speed of what was supposed to be a high-speed train. The solution came only after a significant investment in R&D to redesign the ties of the track to make them aerodynamic.

One way to manage this kind of risk is to stage investments. For instance, various companies now manage new product development using a stage-gate process (figure 2.2). Development goes through stages, and the end of each stage has a gate at which top management evaluates the project. At that point, manage-

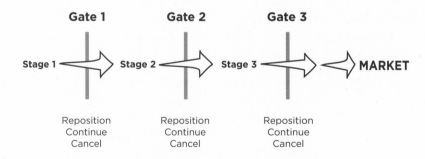

Figure 2.2. The stage-gate process

ment can either give the go-ahead to move the project to the next stage, make changes, or cancel the project altogether. Different companies have different numbers of stages, but all stages serve the same purpose: to periodically review investments with the option to cancel so that an organization can cut losses quickly on investments that aren't working.

Another way for top management to generate continuous improvement is by planning and monitoring progress. Planning yields a set of targets that employees throughout the organization have to meet. Ideally, these targets are challenging but achievable. Henkel CEO Kasper Rorsted, for example, relied heavily on making people more accountable in transforming the company. Accountability was enforced through a culture that emphasized the customer; a transparent evaluation system to identify top and bottom performers; and a balanced incentive system with individual, team, and company incentives. The drive for performance resulted in people throughout the company identifying new opportunities for growth and efficiency.

Pushing for performance can lead people to be more creative, but that pressure needs to come with risk management systems and a balanced culture. Without them, creativity can undermine, rather than support, value creation. For example, Microsoft performance has been average over the last decade—the company's stock price has barely appreciated. Analysts speculating on reasons for this have cited a corporate strategy that follows trends instead of creating new ones, and an evaluation system based on forced ranking—or stack ranking—which encourages people to worry about their own ranking rather than to collaborate to create value.[5]

To avoid the risk of people using their creativity to invent dangerous short cuts, strong codes of conduct are important. These boundary systems or ethical guidelines set limits on what behaviors are acceptable and what kind of activities fall within (and outside of) the approved strategy. Making shared values explicit shapes a healthy culture that supports the creation of economic and social value.[6] Such systems channel organizational energy in the right direction and help deter people from using their creativity to undermine the system.

D emanding targets lead people to be creative in finding incremental innovation opportunities as long as the associated risks are managed.

Giving people challenging yet achievable targets forces them to be creative to improve how they work. But this creativity will remain at the individual level unless mechanisms are put in place to disseminate it. Incremental innovation isn't always about demanding targets—sometimes it's about facilitating and leveraging the creativity that lies dormant within an organization and its networks.

Business Units Can Manage Emergent Improvements

With the right systems in place, it is possible to stimulate and capture incremental innovation throughout the company and its networks. These management systems channel the ingenuity of employees, customers, and almost anybody who is in some way related to the company. When business units successfully manage bottom-up incremental innovation, they integrate creativity from all these sources into a formal innovation process.

Software companies such as Amazon and Google often use A/B experiments, a systematic approach to selecting among competing ideas. By offering various designs of the same web page at the same time to different visitors, companies can monitor which design works best. Marketing companies employ similar approaches for choosing between marketing campaign alternatives. Another example of a business that encourages and manages emergent improvements successfully is Keyence, a Japanese designer and builder of automation devices for factories. The company has devised a process whereby employees spend long periods of time at the factories of its customers, interacting with and observing them. These visits have led to multiple ideas about new products and new ways to serve customers.[7]

Even utilizing a simple tool like a suggestion box requires managing the innovation cycle. Simply hanging up a box (or posting a web page) will not get creativity flowing; the process needs to entice and encourage people to share their ideas. Various tools—from tournaments to exploration trips and interest groups—are intended to stimulate inventiveness, expose people to new experiences, and offer economic and social rewards. The ideas that emerge need to be evaluated, selected from, and ultimately implemented. For company-wide efforts, the management of hundreds or thousands of ideas and their evaluation, selection, and implementation may require a large number of people.

Incremental innovations often lead to small performance improvements, but occasionally they also may mean very large revenues or savings for the organization. In such instances, it can be tempting to commit to further incremental innovation—where business units, after all, excel. But what incremental innovation has working in its favor can almost just as easily work against it.

THE LIMITS OF BUSINESS UNITS

Over the past hundred years, business units have been the preferred organizational structure largely because they deliver value. However, while they are in many cases the best way to execute a strategy, their core advantage becomes their core weakness when industries go through revolutions. Their focus on execution and incremental innovation can crowd out any real opportunity for developing breakthrough innovation.

Business units are built on the assumption that the market will evolve slowly and predictably. Thus, their search for ideas is often local; they frequently look for innovation in technologies and business models close to where they currently are. When industries go through large structural changes, a business unit's intuitive response is often to do what they know best—only more of it, and faster—and to try to protect an old industry structure rather than adapt to the new one. As former Procter and Gamble CEO A. G. Lafley said, "First-time chief executives rarely have much experience with weighting the balance toward a long-term future. Typically, they've been accountable for results only a few months out. Their careers have not depended on bets placed a decade or more into the future."[8]

The company that originally came up with the concept of business units, General Motors, illustrates some of their pros and cons. For decades GM dominated the car industry by playing on the competitive advantage that business units' focus provided. As long as the industry remained within a set of fairly narrow parameters, GM kept winning. But changes in the market—customers demanding new concepts, energy prices skyrocketing, and foreign competitors such as Toyota offering better cost and quality management innovations—challenged GM's leadership position. The inertia of business units to reinforce past winning strategies led to the company's bailout by the US government in 2009. Table 2.3 lists the major limits of the business unit structure.

Table 2.3. Limits of the business unit structure

Defensive attitudes reinforce existing models
Assumes steady and predictable industry evolution
Existing power structures can be sticky
Measures short-term results
Demands predictable and stable results
Execution routines reject radical ideas

Defensive Attitudes within Business Units
Reinforce Existing Business Models

Few companies can quickly adapt to large shifts in their industries. Kodak, the eternal leader in the photography film industry, is another winner-turned-loser because of business units' characteristics. The company dominated film for decades, beating every competitor who entered the industry. But the coming of digital photography ultimately forced Kodak into bankruptcy. As with Nokia and the smart phone, the irony of the Kodak case is that the company was the first to go into digital photography. It created the original digital camera and predicted its eventual success, but the inertia of Kodak's past winning strategy, reinforced by defensive attitudes within its business units, did not allow this breakthrough innovation to grow. The company kept getting better and better at executing for what had become an increasingly small market.

Business Units Assume Steady
and Predictable Industry Evolution

The assumption that industries will move steadily has been true most of the time and in most markets. For example, the structure of the energy industry has remained stable, the rules of the game basically have not altered for decades, and the main players—Shell and Exxon Mobil—have stayed at the top throughout. Why should a particular renewable source of energy upset this solid structure? Alternately, education today looks much as it did two hundred years ago, and some aspects have not changed for thousands of years. Why should we expect something like e-learning to challenge these traditions? From the vantage point of business units—which assume steady and predictable industry evolution—we shouldn't. However, the assumption of slow movement within industries sometimes fails, and when it does, the business unit structure may find itself unable to respond.

Existing Power Structures within Business Units Can Be Sticky

Radical changes in an industry require a new configuration of knowledge. The information that was once at the core of competitive advantage becomes peripheral in the new competitive landscape, while knowledge that before was subordinate now becomes core. Still, several forces fight to maintain the status quo, even if mounting evidence indicates that current strategies are no longer valid. One such force is a company's power structure. The internal power struggle in a particular newspaper in Europe is a case in point. Product market forces were obvious to all top managers: the paper had fired more than 20 percent of the workforce over eighteen months as former readers of print moved to find their news online. The dynamics of the market were clearly changing rapidly, but the paper team—the team that had held the power within the organization for decades—was not ready to let the Internet business dominate. Perceiving the Internet business as a side business since its inception, the paper team decided to rename itself the "Internet team" in a weak attempt to hold onto power.

Business Units Measure Short-Term Results

Another inherent limitation of the business unit design for breakthrough innovation is its short-term orientation. Performance is measured quarterly in the stock markets, and more often internally, and innovation can only be argued for if it delivers on its promise sooner rather than later. Rewards, promotion opportunities, and reputation are tied to short-term results, and managers respond to these incentives by focusing on delivering in the next quarter. A manager from Boeing described this frustration: "I often wonder, if society existed [in the past] as it does today with the media, politicians, and lawyers and managers focused on not missing earnings by two cents per quarter, whether we would have made the advances of the past."[9]

Business Units Demand Predictable and Stable Results

Business units are averse to uncertainty. Investors value predictable and stable results and tend to shy away from volatile assets. Radical ideas are often too uncertain to support stable financial performance, even after using portfolio techniques to limit idiosyncratic risk. Thus, business units often favor innovations low on uncertainty, whose financial returns are predictable. This tendency for business units to favor the safe makes the decisions of the Kodaks and Nokias of the world—to focus on past successes rather than new technologies—seem logical. However, results are predictable and stable only up to a point. When radical market changes occur, the risk aversion of business units can be their downfall.

Execution Routines within Business Units Reject Radical Ideas

The management systems built for execution—budgets, processes, quality control, and sales pipelines—are designed to reduce variation and enhance efficiency. These systems see variation as a problem rather than an opportunity. Deviations from the expected are quickly addressed to bring the process back in line with the plan. The quality of these routines determines the quality of execution in stable times. Even if the industry structure is going through radical changes, execution routines still frequently reinforce the patterns that had been successful in the past—almost as if organizational antibodies rejected change to maintain stability in the body of the organization.[10]

Business units are best designed for predictable industries. Often their response to radical changes in industry structure is to reinforce previously successful strategies—strategies that are becoming obsolete.

BUSINESS UNITS, FUNCTIONAL STRUCTURE, AND BREAKTHROUGH INNOVATION

There is one notable exception to business units' typical inability to create and respond to structural changes: visionary CEOs who go for strategic bets. A strong CEO with a vision to disrupt an industry and the muscle of an execution-oriented company to pursue her radical concept can bring about breakthrough change.

A business unit structure shaped to execute the strategy designed by top managers can deliver on breakthrough innovation if it comes from the top. The best example is Steve Jobs's turnaround of Apple in the late 1990s. The iPod, iTunes, the iPhone, the iPad, and the App Store were all part of the vision of Jobs and a tight group around him. Not only did these developments disrupt current markets and create new ones, they dominated them—in large part because of the quality of the vision and the organization's ability to execute on it. But Steve Jobs at Apple isn't the sole noteworthy case. Lou Gestner at IBM and Sergio Marchionne at Fiat are also leaders whose concepts saved their respective companies. The leader has to be inspiring, trustworthy, and tough enough to break the forces within the company that will react negatively to her vision. But if she gets people to rally behind her, she has an organization that can upset an industry.

Getting the organization to fall in line behind a visionary leader is easier when the company's performance is deteriorating. Apple had just gone through three CEOs before Jobs came back, and the company was viewed as a relic from the early years of the computer industry. Gestner took over when the consensus was that IBM was going to disappear. Marchionne got to the helm when Fiat was losing market share in most of its markets and its cars were being described as dull. In such circumstances, employees and investors agree that change is needed, and they are much more likely to be ready and willing to support the new leader.

No matter how you look at it, the visionary leader is ultimately betting the company on her vision of the future; she succeeds if she has the right vision and her breakthrough innovation creates a new market or upsets an existing one. But breakthrough innovation is a risky business, and more often than not, the turnaround fails to happen. Visionary leaders can have the wrong vision or fail to implement it successfully.

Few leaders have more winning visions than losing ones. Those who do are business geniuses who more often than not get the future right and build it. Geniuses play a pivotal role in all aspects of life; they are outliers who shape the way we live. Many significant advances in society are the outcomes of these visionaries, and they exist in every walk of life—music, architecture, painting, chemistry, biology, and political science. Of course, to implement their vision, most of these people needed both the support of teams and the ability to manage them. Business is no exception.

Business units have a number of advantages, and being able to execute on the vision of a leader is ranked high among them. Unfortunately, most managers are not geniuses, so betting the future of an organization on the vision of a CEO is a risky proposition. In fact, breakthrough innovation is itself quite risky, but it is necessary for the continued growth and survival of an organization. For insight into how risk-averse organizations can learn to thrive in uncertain environments and not-yet markets, we look to those who live and thrive in ambiguity: startups.

Few leaders have successful visions of the future more often than unsuccessful ones. The ones who do bring about breakthrough innovation by leveraging the ability of business units to execute on their vision of the future.

QUALITY OF EXECUTION

- How well does my organization execute compared to similar organizations around the world?
- How is the strategic planning and budgeting process designed? How does it motivate progress?
- How is progress measured in my organization?
- How motivated are the people in my organization?
- Are the management design and culture of my organization demanding yet maintaining a healthy attitude?
- How does my organization manage the various sources of risk?
- How does my organization incorporate emergent improvements?
- What is the role of continuous progress in my organization?

SOURCES OF RADICAL CHANGES IN THE INDUSTRY

- What experiments around the world could challenge the existing industry structure?
- How is my organization tracking these potential sources of radical change?
- What are the main assumptions that drive my organization?
- How hard would it be to shift the mental model of my organization if the industry goes through a radical change?

DRIVING STRUCTURAL CHANGE

- How does my organization support a discovery mentality to lead breakthrough changes?
- How does my organization combine focus on execution and an open approach to experimental breakthrough solutions?
- How does my organization balance the weaknesses of a business unit structure?
- What changes to the existing design of my organization could balance the strengths and limitations of a business unit structure?

The Success of Startups

OVER THE LAST TWENTY YEARS, startup companies have been major players when it comes to breakthrough innovation. Newborn businesses have appeared out of nowhere, upsetting industries, destroying venerable companies that had been around for decades, and creating industries that did not exist before. Amazon in retail distribution and Google in Internet search and many other services are two prominent examples of startups' creative destruction. These companies, each now employing thousands, have excelled both at executing a winning business model and at creating and growing new markets.

It does seem counterintuitive that companies with limited resources—businesses that often rely on external funding from venture capitalists—can so quickly rise to dominate industries. Traditionally, large companies and their R&D departments were the natural repositories of breakthrough innovation. Businesspeople, as well as economists like Joseph Schumpeter and management theorists like Edith Penrose, had nearly accepted that creative destruction had to originate from established players. These players were, after all, the only ones with enough resources to devote financing to breakthrough innovation.

So, what is unique to the way startups operate that has enabled their success in developing breakthrough innovation? And why have some established organizations been able to replicate that kind of innovation when others have failed? A few of the unspoken principles that guide innovation at successful startups include:

- Copy and combine from others
- Learn as quickly and as cheaply as possible
- Manage risk effectively
- Govern transparently
- Execute

None of these principles on its own is enough to foster breakthrough innovation, and each has a unique contribution to a startup's ability to develop breakthrough innovations.

COPY AND COMBINE FROM OTHERS

One quality of successful startups that established companies have only recently caught on to is their openness. Smart entrepreneurs leverage external resources—for building their business models, entrepreneurs grab ideas from everywhere. One obvious example of leveraging outside resources is venture funding; another is technology startups' use of technology developed in universities (who are, in turn, usually happy to see it utilized), or inspired in private and public R&D labs. Startups with less of a technology component also nurture their business models with ideas from colleagues, startups in other countries, and other markets.

"Creativity is the act of connecting things,"[1] and innovation—especially breakthrough innovation—is often about copying and combining existing solutions to create new ones. Different startups use the forces of copying and combining in different ways. For instance, German entrepreneurs Oliver, Marc, and Alexander Samwer have made a routine of replicating US Internet startups in Europe (and have amassed a large fortune in the process).[2] Their first big hit was a copycat of eBay; eBay ultimately had to purchase it when the company decided to go to Europe (doing so was faster and cheaper than building a new eBay from the ground up). While the copycat model has now spread around the world, the Samwer brothers still dominate the European scene, having launched more than one hundred European adaptations of US successes. Their Zappos adaptation alone is estimated to be worth close to $1 billion.

While some like the Samwer brothers rely on copying and adapting, other startups spend more time combining existing ideas to develop their own business models. Many e-commerce startups, for example, bring off-line markets online. What Amazon did for books (and practically every other type of consumer good) Peapod has done for supermarkets, and Zappos for shoes.

Another aspect of the open-to-the-world orientation of many startups is the fact that smart entrepreneurs are the main salespeople of their companies. Because their marketing budget is limited, they are constantly selling the value proposition of their companies. Marc Benioff, the founder of Salesforce.com, took every opportunity he could get to talk about his company. When it was still relatively small, he was interviewed at CNN and CNBC for his views on the economy, and he used these opportunities to promote Salesforce.com. His role as CEO was more like that of an ambassador, salesman, and publicist than that of a traditional CEO. In fact, he was so engaged in his public relations role that violations to the quiet period threatened the initial public offering (IPO) of the company. From the vantage point of innovation behind closed doors, though, it is counterintuitive for these entrepreneurs to be so out in the open. Many entrepreneurs won't describe their ideas for fear of having them copied, but startup CEOs like Benioff preach their gospel whenever they can.

The open attitude of numerous startups is in stark contrast to the closed approach that has been a trademark of many big companies. The "Not Invented Here" syndrome of established companies—whereby advancements developed outside the organization are shunned for that reason—reflects a certain degree of arrogance. Large R&D departments believe that their mastery of certain technologies is unparalleled, while workshops and meetings only reinforce their conviction that outsiders are good, but not superior. Large marketing departments behave similarly—they believe that their market research and market deployment tools are unbeatable. Yet these assumptions have been proven wrong time and time again.

The success of programs like Procter and Gamble's Connect + Develop has forced some established organizations to pay attention to the ways in which startups innovate. Connect + Develop emphasized leveraging external partners throughout the R&D process. However, before it could succeed, Procter and Gamble had to change incentives to reduce the "Not Invented Here" attitude that was pervasive inside the company. One of the more notable changes was to reward employees for identifying licensing opportunities.[3] The program ultimately succeeded in making R&D more efficient, and in systematizing open innovation within the company. Still, critics claim the rate of breakthrough innovation falls short of the program's promises. The lower-than-expected number of breakthroughs, though, may be a result of those external ideas being executed more traditionally.[4]

Creativity derives from copying and combining existing ideas into new ones. Increasing exposure to different environments and a bias toward experimentation support the search for innovation.

Copying and combining often lead to successful startups being founded on unique insights, which is where imagination plays a significant role. For instance, Vente-Privee, a French startup company with sales above two billion euros, is winning the Internet-based luxury-brand market by offering substantial discounts. What Vente-Privee has done that its competitors have not is to capitalize on the idea of treating suppliers—the luxury brands that now dispose of their excess inventory through channels like Vente-Privee—as customers. Where competitors see luxury brands as suppliers and themselves as the customers, Vente-Privee listens to suppliers as it would to any customer and proposes alternatives for disposing of luxury brands' overstock. Rather than having become just another customer, Vente-Privee has basically become a partner in liquidating overstock.[5]

Design thinking and human-centered design have also developed a broad array of techniques to both stimulate and refine ideas, moving from observation and insights to framing the problem, generating ideas, and fine-tuning concepts. For example, Steelcase, an office furnishings manufacturer with a $2 billion market cap, has created a think tank called Workplace Futures. Utilizing human-centered design, Workplace Futures brings together anthropologists, industrial designers, and business strategists to work toward greater insight into customer needs and desires.[6] Table 3.1 summarizes some of the ways in which startups and creative organizations copy and combine to develop new products and business models.

Table 3.1. Copying and combining in startups

Be exposed to different environments
Copy to learn and combine to invent
Translate existing ideas into a new context
Link people and ideas
Communicate and share
Take risks
Play around with new combinations
Leverage networks

LEARN AS QUICKLY AND AS CHEAPLY AS POSSIBLE

Startups' innovation involves little actual planning. Even if the end product of entrepreneurship courses has been the business plan, and the business plan has been offered as the key to venture funding, traditional planning is marginal to the ways in which modern startups function. The more a startup is breaking new ground, the less planning—in the traditional sense of the word—is needed.

Planning is about managing in stable, predictable environments, while breakthrough innovation requires managing in uncertain settings. Startup plans tend to be short-term—just long enough to learn as much about their model as possible before the next learning cycle begins. Figure 3.1 compares the way investments for incremental innovation to further existing competitive advantages are managed to the way in which startups manage their investments. The staged funding of venture capital is a reflection of this second approach.

Plans are typical execution tools designed to deploy a strategy in a known and stable market. In established companies, they define the path forward, and any deviations from them are seen as red flags that require attention. Yet if a breakthrough innovation is

APPROACH FOR ESTABLISHED COMPANIES

APPROACH FOR STARTUPS

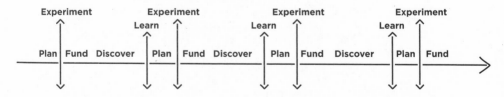

Figure 3.1. Established companies' versus startups' investment management

Breakthrough innovation is less about long-term planning and more about short-term experimentation. It is about exploring, discovering, and crafting an attractive proposition for customers.

managed this way, it morphs into an incremental innovation that fits the existing strategy. Breakthrough innovations can hardly appear as anything other than red flags that need to fall in line when planning takes precedence over exploration and discovery.

Entrepreneurs do not pretend to plan their future. And honestly, how could they? Often they don't even know if their value proposition has customers who are willing to pay for it—and many times their initial plans are wrong! Business plans force them to think about who is most likely to be attracted to their proposition, what the shape of the minimum viable product will be, how the value proposition will reach the customer, and whether there is economic value to be generated. A business plan is a tool to organize a thought process and to explain it to outsiders, but the entrepreneur knows that she needs to move to the market to truly test her ideas. Endlessly tweaking spreadsheets and business plan details are frequently ways to avoid the real test of the market.

For example, a Silicon Valley–based startup in supply chain management software had calculated that its market was mostly made up of medium-size firms. The company's impression became even stronger when a reputed management consultant validated it. However, the market did not exist. The selling cycles were long and the margins were thin. Somewhat serendipitously, a software manager from a large company approached the startup's booth at a trade fair. He was interested in the software, and in a few months, the large company became a customer. This lucky encounter served the startup well, and it eventually succeeded in shifting its marketing efforts to large companies.

Startups experiment. Because breakthrough innovation is

Table 3.2. Learning fast and cheap in startups

Identify critical uncertainties
Design experiments to reduce critical uncertainties for the lowest cost
Be sensitive to the results
Use the results to adapt the innovation and inform future experiments
Cycle through experiment-learn-experiment as quickly and as cheaply as possible

about managing ignorance (rather than managing knowledge, as in incremental innovation), the way to learn is through confronting assumptions concerning a market with the reality of that market. The right technology and the right business model are discovered and shaped through smart experiments. A successful breakthrough innovation is not simply an ingenious idea, but an entire process of discovery and crafting.

In many ways, working toward breakthrough innovation is not that different from developing breakthrough science (in fact, in some cases, it *is* breakthrough science). Scientists have an idea that they test and reformulate over the course of many experiments, each carefully designed to deliver the most value from their effort. Sometimes they succeed in developing something new, while other times they end up dropping the idea altogether. Entrepreneurs are in a similar business of discovery—they must design experiments to discover the needs of their clients, the business proposition that best suits those clients, and how to get that proposition to them. "Planning" in this setting revolves around what can be done to learn the most in the shortest period possible for the smallest investment. Nonetheless, failure is an intrinsic part of the process of discovery, both in science and in business innovation.[7] Table 3.2 summarizes some of the main elements of learning fast and cheap.

MANAGE RISK EFFECTIVELY

Without the security (however illusory) afforded by planning far in advance, innovating in the context of a startup is about risk management—it is about a few large wins and lots of smaller failures. Venture capitalists invest in multiple companies knowing that no more than 20 percent of them will succeed. It would be nice to know beforehand which 20 percent this will be (and thus have a 100 percent success rate), but the journey of discovering and crafting breakthrough innovation is plagued with wrong turns and dead ends.

Entrepreneurs themselves have realized that success is largely a numbers game. As a result, many of them are becoming serial entrepreneurs, developing their entrepreneurial career along several startups. But while starting several companies increases the chances of success, it means that entrepreneurs need to be able to quickly test whether an idea has potential. If they determine that a particular idea is a failure, they then scrap it and move on to the next one. Figure 3.2 illustrates how the number of ideas shrinks as experiments identify winning assumptions and discard the ones that prove to be wrong.

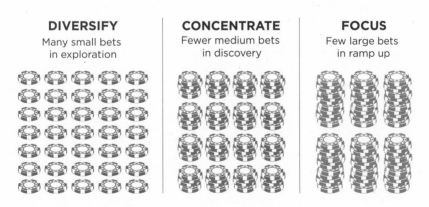

DIVERSIFY
Many small bets
in exploration

CONCENTRATE
Fewer medium bets
in discovery

FOCUS
Few large bets
in ramp up

Figure 3.2. The numbers game of innovation

The need to rapidly test and assess concepts and ideas, how-ever, does not preclude passion. Entrepreneurs are extremely pas-sionate, but they do not let that passion blind them. For example, one entrepreneur who ended up selling his Internet-based com-pany (he controlled 100 percent of the equity) for several million dollars failed more than a few times before finding an idea that worked. In fact, he failed so often, his friends made a game out of listening to him recount his failures. The idea that eventually worked for him was unplanned. Having bought some real estate to rent, he built a web page to advertise his property. Soon he found that other people with apartments to rent wanted to use his website, so he happily worked with them to advertise their listings. He then realized that providing a web presence for short-term rentals was a much bigger business opportunity than simply renting out his own property. From that accidental discovery, the company is now present in more than one hundred cities around the world.

The startup model requires that people believe in their idea beyond the potential economic returns. Although the economics are important, the willingness to work long hours, to multi-task, and to fail several times before finding the successful path reflects a commitment beyond money. As one entrepreneur described it, being an entrepreneur means choosing three out of five of the following objectives:[8]

1. Build a great company
2. Spend time with family
3. Stay fit
4. Get rest, sleep, and personal time
5. Maintain friendships

Yet, as quick as entrepreneurs are to test their ideas, they are equally quick to pivot or discard them altogether. For example, Scripted.com, a successful Silicon Valley–based company, began as a company developing software for script writers (under the

Table 3.3. Managing risk in startups

Diversify risk
Understand risk: what is critical to the innovation
Plan to manage risk
Test main assumptions fast; move on or pivot if they don't work
Don't let passion blind you to reality
Be alert—opportunities may lie on the sidelines of results

original name Scripped.com).[9] The initial idea of the founders—Sunil Rajaraman, Ryan Buckley, and Zachary Freer—was to democratize script writing and make Hollywood more accessible to new talent in the process. The initial idea had traction, but not enough to become the large company the founders envisioned. So they pivoted their model to become a website that provides easy access to top-quality writing. While this model proved to be more attractive, the response to it didn't satisfy the ambitions of the young entrepreneurs. They pivoted again, this time to supply writing to large companies in the form of managing blogs and Twitter accounts. Then they expanded into offering video and photos, and still further into marketing strategies. Scripted.com remains one company, but at least three business models were tested over a four-year period. Table 3.3 lists how startups manage the inherent risk of breakthrough innovation.

GOVERN TRANSPARENTLY

Startups and traditional organizations often differ to a great degree in terms of organizational governance. Whereas business units may seem to exist in silos within an organization, the interests of the various parties governing a startup are transparent: managers want to get as much support as possible to succeed, investors want the company to succeed to maximize returns, and independent directors contribute to success through their particular expertise. This sort of transparency helps facilitate communication, and interaction is frequent—both informally and formally—during board meetings and in between board meetings.

Good boards are diverse and provide a set of perspectives on monitoring performance that goes beyond narrow financial and nonfinancial measures. Board members bring with them their expertise, but they also bring access to their networks—managers, potential customers and partners, lawyers, accounting firms, and individual and corporate investors. Everybody seated at the board table is interested in the success of the company, and each one contributes a different point of view to enrich the discussion. Plans are more like sketches, and deviations—rather than being seen as problems that need to be dealt with—can be taken as opportunities to improve the business model, branch into unfamiliar markets, or integrate new technologies.

Successful governance brings together an experienced and diverse group of people willing to contribute to the best of their abilities to the success of the startup.

Boards meet frequently to follow the evolution of the company and offer their insights and networks. Plans are useful reference points, but they take the back seat to the reality of the situation to better favor success. Initially, plans outline the expected outcomes of experiments that will shape the business model. As the startup progresses and execution becomes more important, plans incorporate quantitative and financial targets. At these stages, plans allow the board to more easily judge whether the management team can execute well enough to quickly grow the company.

Table 3.4. Governing startups

Focus on success
Have transparent objectives
Communicate frequently
Provide access to networks
Plan detailed experiments, not targets to be accomplished
Give discovery priority over plans

Board members are often senior people in the entrepreneurial community and industry. Any breakthrough innovation effort will face large uncertainties, and having senior people on the board provides at least four advantages: 1) access to knowledge; 2) access to networks that facilitate speed and efficiency; 3) credibility facing potential partners, suppliers, and customers; and 4) support and stability through any rough moments. Table 3.4 summarizes the elements of governance within startups.

EXECUTE

Another characteristic of successful startups is attention to detail. Attention to detail in startups is not about executing on a complex plan, as it is in established companies, because there is no strategic plan to implement. It's more about carefully designing and realizing the experiments that inform the important discovery process. Still, at the end of the day, innovation is about execution. In science, researchers who make great discoveries are smart, but they are also careful in devising and carrying out experiments. In startups, entrepreneurs who create great companies are smart, but they are similarly careful in designing and executing their own experiments.

Winners in the entrepreneurship world are those who execute

57

better. Execution has two sides to it: creating and running experiments, and growing the startup. Failing at either will undermine the possibilities of success. As the startup grows, execution becomes more aligned with the traditional execution of an established company—focusing on incremental innovation and operational efficiency.

Successful startups go through discovery-execution cycles more quickly than do their competitors, and they often discover the winning model faster through smarter and better discovery. For example, Trovit is a vertical aggregator that dominates the main search verticals in Europe and Latin America. When it was founded, Trovit competed against more than fifteen other startups pursuing the same business. In every single market, Trovit eventually grabbed the leadership position because of the company's ability to execute. Its management better facilitated the process of discovery, and then followed up by more skillfully executing the business model: effectively utilizing Internet marketing tools such as search engine optimization (SEO) to attract traffic and offer more relevant results.

LEARNING FROM THE ACTIVITIES OF STARTUP INNOVATION

Successful startups grow by shifting from discovery and experimentation into execution and incremental innovation. The process of innovation can be visualized as a set of overlapping activities (figure 3.3). Not necessarily clear cut or sequential, the activities will involve varying elements for different products, services, and industries.

Stimulate. High-growth startups generally emerge from intense environments, with Silicon Valley being the leader. In regions where diversity mixes with passion, constant exchange, freedom to fail, and easy networking, ideas move quickly, allowing people and organizations to combine them and spot new opportunities. Resources abound, and seed money is available for initial steps. People go from one networking event to a pre-startup work-

---

STARTUP MODEL

STIMULATE   ENTICE   SELECT   DISCOVER   GROW   EXIT

Figure 3.3. Activities of startup innovation

ing on a new idea. Open incubators and accelerators provide mentoring and support. Universities are often magnets for startup activity. Having a great number and variety of resources in a relatively small area makes a fertile ecosystem for developing breakthrough innovations.

Entice. Ideas that get positive response from the market are quickly picked up by that same ecosystem of partners. Lawyers, accountants, venture capitalists, and executive search companies supply startups with resources important for running a business but peripheral to developing the core ideas of the startups. They also provide access to networks, which permits startups to build relationships with established companies, governments, and international markets. For example, Y Combinator in Silicon Valley is an initiative that attracts entrepreneurs. Over the course of a few months, entrepreneurs are heavily coached by top people in the valley, given ample resources, and put through an intense discovery process. Companies such as Airbnb.com and Dropbox are just a couple of Y Combinator's alumni.

Select. The greater business ecosystem selects where to invest talent and money, and risk is allocated at this stage. In general, venture capitalists only invest in one out of several dozen startups with whom they've had contact. Most startups simply are not attractive enough and do not survive. Venture capitalists often have a set of criteria that defines the boundaries of where they look for opportunities. For instance, Redpoint Ventures in Silicon Valley focuses on early rounds within the Internet and broadband space; thus, most of their three hundred–plus investments are in this space.

Discover. Going after breakthrough innovation means facing uncertainty on multiple fronts. For technology-heavy startups, the initial concerns center on technology, while business model uncertainties may be relatively few. For instance, since the exit strategy for a biotech startup is often a sale of the business to a pharmaceutical company, the uncertainty inherent in a biotech startup largely involves technology. As the importance of technology decreases, uncertainties move to the different segments of the business model. Financial Engines, a startup company founded to leverage finance research on portfolio management, went through five business models before it discovered a business-to-business approach that made it successful. While some lucky entrepreneurs put all the pieces together the first time around, most try different combinations before they get it right (or discard the idea). The discovery process does not have a specific timeline and does not go through specific milestones.

Grow. Once a startup discovers a winning business model, attention to detail shifts away from experimentation to scaling up quickly, replicating the formula that works, and executing faster than competitors. These skills differ from those required in previous activities, and the same person or persons may not have them. Growth is really more about speed and efficiency than it is about discovery. It is not as much about creativity as it is about execution. It is also not as much about breakthrough innovation as it is about incremental innovation, and here is where many startups struggle. However, growth is critical: the faster it is, the less time the window is open for competitors to enter the market. At this point, the startup begins to transform itself into an established company—an inevitable transformation if the startup wants to fully capture its value.

Exit. The final activity of innovation in successful startups is to capture the value of the innovation. Most startups are a one-innovation company: they have an idea, attract resources, go through the market's somewhat Darwinian selection process, dis-

Table 3.5. Learning from the activities
of startup innovation

Stimulate creativity—a rich environment
is more likely to generate great ideas

Make resources available to experiment

Reward people who take risks

Let market forces select the winners

Don't stop discovering too soon

Adapt management talent to the needs
of the company

cover how to make the idea work, and grow it. Successful start-ups—the very few that reach this last stage—often exit through selling the business. Established companies buy them and integrate their solutions into the larger business, thus freeing up the value. In some instances, the startup remains as an independent company, either as a private company or more often as a public one through an IPO. These independent companies become established players that ultimately face the same decisions as incumbents in their industry: How should we play the incremental-breakthrough game? Will the industry evolve gradually, or will it face radical structural changes? How do we get breakthrough innovation?

Table 3.5 summarizes the key points to learn from startup innovation.

LEARNING FROM THE CREATION OF SCIENCE

World-class research institutes are a constant source of new breakthrough technologies. While they do not encounter the pressure that companies have of needing to develop a product that will make it to the market, their organizations still offer valuable lessons about how to organize for breakthrough innovation.

The Weizmann Institute is a leading research institution in Israel. Its approach to advancing science is similar to that of other research universities throughout the world. As researchers will tell you, discovery happens in two ways. The first is goal-driven: a problem or a market opportunity appears, and an organization invests resources with the goal of developing a solution. The second—and the one that research institutions pursue most often—is curiosity-driven. Curiosity-driven research relies on freedom and serendipity, and their intersection is often where breakthrough ideas emerge. Researchers investigate certain questions because intuition and curiosity tell them that something relevant is to be gained from their inquiry. Most breakthrough technologies occur not in search of a solution to a particular problem but without a specific application in view. Whereas specific goals tend to narrow your mind, curiosity opens it (figure 3.4).

For example, a researcher at the Weizmann Institute, Ernesto Joselevich, discovered a fundamental property of nanotubes—the basic building block of nanotechnologies—through a combination of serendipity and curiosity. One of his doctoral students bought a sapphire for an experiment. Because of budget con-

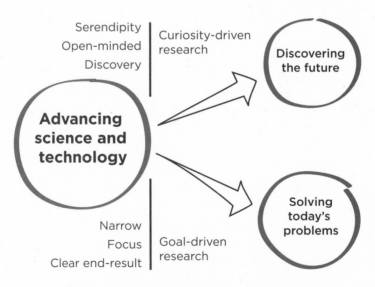

Figure 3.4. Two approaches to research in science

straints, he got it from the cheapest supplier he could find, so the sapphire was not perfectly cut. The results of the experiments made no sense: the nanotubes were forming structures that were not the ones the particular theory they were testing predicted. The researchers kept asking why until they found the imperfection in the sapphire, and in turn the experiment. The next challenge became to understand why these unusual structures were forming with the slightly tilted sapphire. The answer to this further question led them to their groundbreaking discovery.

Innovation can be goal-driven or curiosity-driven. The former often leads to searches around a narrow set of options. The latter inspires more unique discoveries.

Daniel Zajfman, president of the Weizmann Institute, described curiosity-driven discovery: "If you see something that you don't understand, but you try to understand it, you will be able to do things that you did not imagine. This is how we work. We do not focus on the problem, we are driven by curiosity. Problem solving never creates solutions for problems of the future."[10]

The most important decisions at the Weizmann Institute concern hiring. Since the raw input for creating new science and technologies is very smart, well-trained, and passionate people, hiring is carefully done to minimize mistakes. The organization then only needs to provide the resources and an environment in which researchers can thrive. "Hiring the right people is the first condition for success," said Zajfman, "The overriding concern remains summarized in three words: talent, talent, talent."

Although hiring good staff members is the number-one priority, compensation and having the necessary tools are also important. Researchers get paid a competitive salary and are given access to all the resources they need. While the institute works

Table 3.6. Comparing curiosity-driven and goal-driven innovation

CURIOSITY-DRIVEN RESEARCH (breakthrough innovation)	GOAL-DRIVEN RESEARCH (incremental innovation)
The result is the discovery	The goal is the result
Solve the problems of the future	Solve today's problems
Don't underestimate serendipity	Don't underestimate focus
Constantly ask why	Constantly pursue the end goal
Mistakes are learning opportunities	Avoid mistakes
Share the value generated	Reward meeting the goal
Hire talented, passionate, and curious people	Hire talented, passionate, and focused people
Provide as many resources as possible	Closely monitor resources
Assess progress through experts' evaluation	Assess progress through milestones

to discover the technologies of the future, it emphasizes market orientation as well. YEDA Research and Technology Company is a market-focused department run by businesspeople that commercializes the science developed at the institute. It also manages all intellectual property–related aspects to make sure that the full value of innovations developed within the institute stays with the organization. Royalties are a significant source of funding for the institute, but they are shared with the researchers who developed the technologies. Researchers thus share in the value that their science creates in the market. As a consequence, the institute houses not only Nobel Prize winners but also a few millionaires. Table 3.6 compares these two approaches to research.

A number of elements of successful startups are well suited to dealing with ambiguous markets and turning relatively few resources into disruptive, breakthrough innovations. Established organizations, though challenged by uncertain environments, still have advantages in terms of execution, operational efficiency, and access to resources. Both breakthrough innovation and incremental innovation are important for organizations' continued success. In the next chapter, we'll look at how companies can overcome the innovation paradox by leveraging both the breakthrough potential of startups and the resources and execution ability of established organizations.

QUESTIONS FOR ACTION

EXPERIENCE FROM STARTUPS

- What experience does my organization have in working with startups?
- Does my organization stimulate people to have a diverse set of experiences?
- Does my organization make an effort to bring together different perspectives?
- What is the role of goal-driven and curiosity-driven innovation in my organization?
- How does my organization manage the transition from discovery to execution?

APPLYING THE STARTUP PRINCIPLES

- How does the environment in my organization inspire people to copy and combine ideas?
- How are learning and experimenting perceived in my organization?
- How does my organization manage the risk associated with innovation?
- How does my organization bring in expertise from the outside to support innovation?

QUESTIONS FOR ACTION

- What is my organization's structure for supervising innovation efforts?
- How would I change the management of my organization to incorporate ideas from successful startups?

ACTIVITIES OF STARTUP INNOVATION

- Does the innovation process in my organization move through clearly defined activities?
- How does the innovation combine the different activities?
- Which activities are weakest in my organization's innovation process? Which are strongest?
- How can I redesign the innovation process of my organization to better facilitate breakthrough innovation?

4.
The Startup Corporation
The New Kid on the Block

GOOGLE WAS FOUNDED on the benefits of a better search engine algorithm, and its search engine is still its largest business. But Google hasn't just sat back on its haunches, content to be a leader in search. On the contrary, the company has added numerous new businesses, most of them derived from the ingenuity of its people. (Of course, the company has also leveraged ideas from the outside with acquisitions such as Double Click, AdMob, Keyhole—the initial insight into Google Earth—Grand Central, and Motorola.) Gmail, Google News, Google Maps, Google Docs, Google Car, Google Glass, Android, and Chrome are some of the well-known innovations to come out of Google.

How does Google foster an environment ripe with ideas like these? To start, the company gives its engineers 20 percent free time (one day a week) to pursue their own projects—a concept shared with 3M but originally begun at universities, where faculty members traditionally have had one day per week to interact with outside organizations. The objective of giving engineers regular free time is to allow them to be exposed to new ideas, and to encourage curiosity-driven work. Free-time projects are exploratory adventures not necessarily tied to the business model, and Google believes that letting people pursue their passions makes them both more productive and more innovative.

To further the cross-fertilization of ideas, Google encourages people to interact with each other, and to share and nurture their thoughts at lunch, through the company's intranet, or in meetings to specifically discuss these projects. Ideas that gain enough momentum receive additional funding, while exceptional ones reach Google Creative Lab, which ultimately involves users in testing to better focus product function and design.

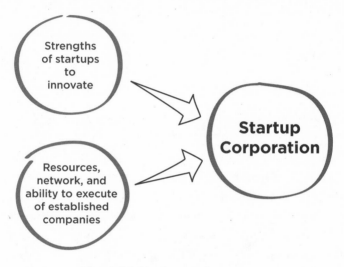

Figure 4.1. The Startup Corporation

By providing workers a certain amount of unstructured free time to explore their own areas of interest and expertise, Google has engineered an environment in which thinking radically is not only allowed but encouraged. Once an idea approaches becoming a viable product, it has the might of Google behind it. By leveraging established organizations' resources and ability to execute with startups' insights into breakthrough development, organizations can fight through the innovation paradox and ultimately grow. This is the promise of the Startup Corporation.

The Startup Corporation blends the innovation philosophy of successful startups with the experience, access to resources, and network of an established company (figure 4.1). The Startup Corporation is designed to create complex innovations that combine multiple partners, knowledge fields, and networks. Startups cannot develop these kinds of innovations, simply because they lack access to the resources and capabilities that established companies have.

BEYOND THE SUCCESS OF STARTUPS

With the abundant opportunities that web-based technologies offered to change social interaction in the 1990s, many large companies—the traditional repositories of breakthrough innovation—were disrupted by the way startups brought breakthrough innovation to the market. Startups' superior model for developing breakthrough innovation in certain settings is one reason for this phenomenon, but the unwillingness of established companies to change their own approach to innovation is another. Since the emergence of the R&D lab in the 1950s, the desire for breakthrough innovation had been satisfied by resources going into these labs—isolated from the rest of the company—and the hope that they would eventually generate breakthrough ideas.

As more companies came to terms with the success of startups in developing breakthroughs and the limits of their own approaches, they started to experiment. Some began by trying to transform into a big startup, only to find that the effort failed. Established companies were too large, too bureaucratic, too slow, and too focused on maintaining the status quo to beat startups at their own game. While becoming a startup was not the answer, learning from startups was a step in the right direction.

Some sizable companies reproduce the startup environment as much as possible. Medwinds, for example, is a European startup that designs clothing inspired by Mediterranean traditions. Their offices have the feeling and energy level of a startup company's.

Yet Camper, one of the world's largest shoe brands, controls 100 percent of Medwinds' equity. Even so, the company behaves as a startup; its people are committed to building a clothing brand on the Internet. They are constantly learning, and they are carefully executing on every aspect of the business.

Medwinds quickly learned that being part of a large group had limitations, but they also discovered a number of advantages. Belonging to a large group allows Medwinds to focus all of its attention on the brand. The company's finance and administration are outsourced to Camper's sophisticated departments. Camper also manages suppliers and manufacturers, and lets Medwinds "rent" a corner in one of Camper's distribution centers.

Building a clothing brand on the Internet proved to be more challenging than anticipated, so Medwinds eventually borrowed the established brand of its parent company. Having a large company behind a startup increases its probability of succeeding compared to its chances as a stand-alone startup. Camper now designs, manufactures, and distributes Medwinds' shoes so the startup company can focus on e-commerce. While Medwinds' team does not enjoy the equity incentive that is a trademark of startup companies, it does have the security that the backing of an established company provides. The team knows it can take risks because the economic resources of Camper are there to support it.

The new kid on the block—the Startup Corporation—looks like a startup and feels like a startup, but it is a more powerful concept because of its fast access to global resources. What Schumpeter and Penrose argued was the original advantage of big companies—the large amount of resources available for experimenting—is being combined with elements of successful startups.

Whereas startups have something of an edge when it comes to nimble, curiosity-driven development, established companies maintain a significant advantage in bringing breakthrough inno-

E stablished companies have unique access to a vast array of knowledge, technologies, and networks, making them best equipped to develop complex breakthrough innovation.

vation to the market. Some startups may be able to outsource noncore aspects of the business, such as finance and administration, but they do not have large companies' access to established brands, an array of technologies, and a global network of partners for marketing, sales, production, and distribution.

The greatest business opportunities often require complex solutions. The environment, health care, energy, education, smart cities, and security are several of the complicated systems that large organizations are best suited to tackle effectively. In such cases as energy and health care, the US government takes the lead in stimulating the search for the breakthrough innovations that will shift industry structures. While governments have the power to change the rules of the game, they do not have the management capabilities and access to technologies and markets to make breakthrough innovations happen. Established companies do.[1] These organizations can activate a diverse set of networks to have them collaborate and coordinate their efforts in addressing substantial challenges. Their key competitive advantage is their ability to manage complexity.

Established companies that attempt to imitate startups fail because they chase the wrong type of innovation. Startups are still best suited to generate breakthrough product innovations, and the Startup Corporation will hardly be able to beat them at their game. The sweet spot for the Startup Corporation is different— although it can devise breakthrough products, its largest impact lies in creating and growing markets that require the joining of diverse resources, knowledge, and networks (table 4.1).

Table 4.1. Comparing the Startup and the Startup Corporation

STARTUP	STARTUP CORPORATION
Copies and combines from people around founders to identify ideas that will lead to creating and redefining products	Leverages internal insights and rich networks around the company to generate ideas that will change industries
Learns as fast and as cheaply as possible through smart experiments to lower uncertainty	Sets up structures to support experimentation by leveraging internal resources and external networks
Focuses governance on the success of the startup, with constituencies bringing their assets to support the company	Receives support from top management through attention, funding, and high-quality resources
Adapts a management approach appropriate to the particular needs of the startup stage	Combines market and internal forces throughout the innovation process
Executes flawlessly and quickly once the foundations of the innovation are fully defined	Integrates into the established company to leverage its global presence and networks

Consider Nokia Money's effort to offer banking through mobile phones to the underserved rural and less affluent urban populations of countries such as India and China. The economic rents of these segments of the population are rapidly growing, yet they do not use the banking system. The size and income growth of these segments will mean a market in the billions of dollars, but establishing a business requires more than mobile technology. Nokia had to activate a network of players from banking institutions to government agencies as well as a complex distribution network for people to learn and use the new system. Because of the complexity of the business model and the need to leverage so many players, the business could only be built by a company with the resources, reputation, and credibility to bring it all together.[2]

The idea of innovating beyond specific products to address

large-scale, complex issues—actually, innovating at the systems level—has attracted venture capitalists, too. Opportunities for substantial, lucrative businesses or major social changes often require innovating in multiple dimensions and seldom involve simply formulating a new product. Of course, venture capitalists still support one-product startups that feed into more extensive system innovation efforts through acquisitions, but they are also looking at their investment portfolios as ways of constructing innovation ecosystems—ecosystems in which each startup in their portfolio contributes to creating a new industry.[3] For example, the effort of venture capital firms in renewable energy is geared toward founding a new industry rather than designing unrelated single products. While the goals of the Startup Corporation are often broader in scope than those of startups, a few things may be learned from the strengths of startups.

ADOPTING THE STRENGTHS OF STARTUPS

The first characteristic of successful startups that some established companies have adopted is dropping the "Not Invented Here" syndrome in favor of an orientation closer to "Happily Learning from Everywhere"—recognizing the value of copying and combining, as well as acquiring tools that fit the innovation ecosystem. This trend has crystallized in the concept of open innovation, in which established companies benefit from leveraging not only the insights of their employees but also those of the outside world. Most large companies have subscribed to this idea, although some "organizational antibodies"—organizational attitudes and actions that dismiss efforts that do not directly sustain existing strategies—have occasionally delayed its adoption.[4]

Established companies now understand that innovation, rather than being a secretive activity relegated to the R&D department, includes copying and combining ideas from both within and outside the organization. For example, one of the policies credited for A. G. Lafley's turnaround of Proctor and Gamble was the transformation from a "Not Invented Here" culture into a culture open to external ideas. A stated objective of his was to get more than 50 percent of the company's innovations from outside sources—up from 15 percent.[5] Another initiative was to make innovation a structured process—not so much that innovation was restricted, but enough that it could be managed.

Planning as a Discovery Path

Moving from the concept of planning as a blueprint for execution to planning as a discovery path is another change to the innovation approach that established companies gleaned from startups. Creating a startup based on a breakthrough idea is about planning to discover and better understand how a business model will work. The discovery process consists of experimenting to resolve uncertainties and learning as much as possible for a small investment of time and resources.

This same concept of discovery is deeply ingrained in scientific research. Each experiment plays a role in the pursuit of breakthrough knowledge, and each one shapes how future experiments will be designed. Think about the discovery process of active molecules in pharmaceutical research. The process contains significant scientific uncertainty, as most of the tested molecules do not work in the ways researchers would like. When uncertainty is high and failure is likely, the objective is to move as quickly and as cheaply through experiments as possible, with the results of every experiment informing the design of the next.

Operating under the idea of planning as discovery rather than the idea of planning as execution runs counter to the largely incremental philosophy of business units. However, for breakthrough innovation to happen, it needs to be nurtured and protected from the short-term demands of business units. Solutions often require creating separate structures in which innovations can grow. Sometimes business unit managers are able to develop a culture in which initial steps concerning new ideas can be taken below the radar screen of short-term forces. Yet the pressures of business unit goals make this feat hard to achieve.

S trategic discoveries need organizations
adapted to a unique balance between
discovery and execution. Tilting the equilibrium
one way or another will lower the chances of
discovery being successfully brought to market.

Without transitioning into a discovery mode, business units may still successfully generate ideas but manage them as incremental. The planning that goes into incremental processes is about predicting the future, and the opportunities that might have started with the potential for breakthrough are transformed into incremental innovations.

Combining Forces for Strategic Discoveries

More companies have seen their fortunes sour because they kept reinforcing a winning business model that had lost its edge than because they took too many risks. Another aspect of the startup environment that established companies are adopting is risk management. A portfolio approach to managing innovation efforts—balancing incremental and breakthrough innovation—takes advantage of company size to lower overall risk. Some organizations are taking a tip from venture capitalists, embracing the idea that while breakthrough innovation requires both skills and vision, it is also a numbers game. The risk associated with working toward strategic discoveries requires investing in several projects to increase the chance of winning as a portfolio.

In addition to risk management, openness, and learning quickly and cheaply, another important lesson from successful startups is the benefit of looking at innovation not as a single task but as various activities that must be combined. Innovation processes have been depicted in different ways, but they always include divergence-convergence stages.[6] Divergence stages encourage thinking outside of the box, challenging assumptions, and exploring wild ideas. Convergence stages focus on synthesizing the outcomes of divergence stages.

For example, design thinking in product development at companies like Frog Design, Design Continuum, or IDEO is based on the concept of exploratory steps being followed by periods of synthesis. The objective is to stimulate ideas, bringing together myriad perspectives from people exposed to various rich environments. Teams in these organizations include biologists, medical doctors, engineers, designers, businesspeople, teachers, and ethnographers—anyone whose experience increases opportunities for combining and cross-pollinating. Observing and imagining in a variety of environments with numerous perspectives stimulate new ideas. Synthesizing these observations and dreams into insights leads to problem framing, and the ideas generated as a response to the problem feed a whole new cycle of divergent thinking. Eventually, this new knowledge is synthesized into early experiments that further inform the discovery process. Each of these activities benefits from diverse perspectives; bringing in experts, customers, suppliers, or even people unrelated to the issue at hand often helps.

Balancing Market Forces and Open Networks

Breakthrough innovation in established organizations balances internal resources and open networks, taking advantage of their suite of global assets. These organizations combine tangible resources such as capital and access to suppliers and distribution channels with intangible ones such as brands, relationships, knowledge, and management. Having recognizable brands provides credibility and clout for customers and partners, and can

---

Strategic discoveries benefit from balancing market and company forces, internal resources and knowledge, and open networks.

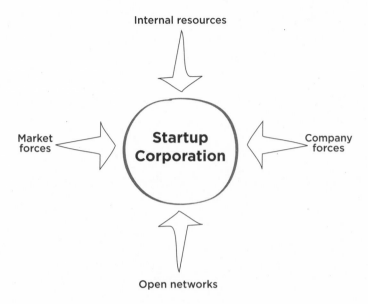

Figure 4.2. Balancing competing forces

help lower their aversion to trying new products and services. Global supply chains provide almost instant access to very large markets. Established companies also have access to a vast number of networks, bringing together a potentially powerful combination of capabilities. The ability to manage and relate these networks is a significant competitive advantage.

While the innovation process that startups use is largely dependent on market forces and startups' ability to leverage external networks, the Startup Corporation also joins internal resources and company forces (figure 4.2). Whether innovation happens within a startup or an established organization, the process includes various activities, and it always needs to be managed. Each activity shares the back and forth, the push and pull, inherent in designing a new solution.

Managing the Stages of Breakthrough Innovation
Activities in the innovation process leverage both insights from internal resources and contributions from external networks.

Furthermore, they balance market and company forces. Market forces reproduce the kind of selection that takes place in competitive markets, and the innovation process needs the creativity of markets as well as the destruction that happens within them. One typical effect of lowering market forces within organizations is that projects with little promise can be kept alive for too long.

Established organizations often do not have an encompassing view of the entire innovation process. This incomplete view leads them to invest in certain, usually early, parts of the process and leave other parts largely unmanaged. The result is a lack of innovation, which then gets blamed on the organization's inherent inability to innovate rather than attributed to mismanagement.

The activities of breakthrough innovation in the Startup Corporation are related to the innovation activities of startups as they go from inception to market (figure 4.3). These activities need unique leaders who question, observe, experiment, network, and associate—up to 50 percent more than do their peers.[7] Whereas creative leaders rely on intuition and inspiration to take on strategic bets, strategic discoveries require the nurturing and support of creative people throughout the company. The type of people

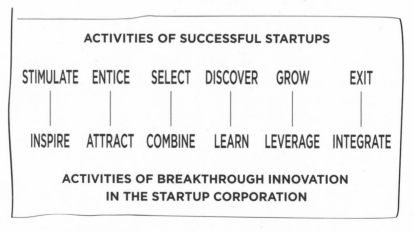

Figure 4.3. The activities of breakthrough innovation

hired (whether they have similar backgrounds and passions or if "weird" people come in) is key.[8] And if an organization truly wants to benefit from the inventiveness of people in its ranks, its environment needs to be conducive to transforming such creativity into valuable opportunities.

STAGE ONE: INSPIRE

Creativity includes combining many existing ideas to devise novel ones. The likelihood of new combinations happening depends on having an environment rich in diverse perspectives, and then providing vehicles for these perspectives to cross-pollinate. Reebok, for example, borrowed the technology for the cushioning of one of its best-selling shoes from intravenous fluid bags, and the microstructures of butterfly wings inspired a revolutionary color display technology at Qualcomm.[9]

As is true of any other aspect of an organization, cross-pollination of ideas and diverse perspectives needs to be managed. Creating the right environment, both physical and cultural, is fundamental. At Procter and Gamble Europe, for example, employees go to a playroom to think and work on new ideas. The colorful room contains movable furniture and various things to draw and build. It offers a very different experience from the corporate environment. Setting up places for people from different backgrounds to meet and exchange ideas can have a profound effect on the type and quality of innovation an organization develops. In this spirit, Toyota encourages frequent interaction among employees, suppliers, and dealers and urges everyone to use formal feedback processes to constantly improve operations.

In contrast to startups—where the stimulus to innovate comes from the entrepreneurial environment—a large corporation needs to design its environments and structures to inspire people. Otherwise, short-term pressures absorb all their attention, and the likelihood of developing breakthrough innovations internally diminishes. Johnson & Johnson planted a flag in an old industrial building in a trendy New York neighborhood when it decided to build a design and creativity division.[10] Software companies frequently make part of their products available to outsiders in an effort to open their own innovation processes to outside ideas. Gaming companies cultivate active forums of users to identify ideas from people deeply engaged in the game's experience. Companies such as Dell, HP, and Netflix launch challenges to customers and outside parties and fund external research to benefit from ideas from outside their organizations.

I n contrast to startups where the stimulus to create is embedded in the forces of markets, established companies need to design how their employees will use their creativity.

In a study of creativity, we looked at how large fashion firms set up the environment of their designers. Drawing rooms and design processes were not as free and unstructured as one might think; rather, different companies used different ways to both inspire creativity in and delineate boundaries for creative people. Fashion companies structure the creative process with two elements: first, an environment that is inspiring yet consistent with the theme of the collection; second, clearly defined boundaries for the team. The confluence of these two elements leads to the development of very different types of collections with different degrees of creativity.

Freedom in fashion design draws on a wide set of resources for creativity: time, slacks in the design team, textures, design complexity, color, theme, and, of course, whether or not to break from existing patterns. Companies competing in lower segments leverage market research and past best-sellers, while companies in prêt-à-porter trust the instincts of their chief designers to identify the next big fashion proposition. Prêt-à-porter relies on exter-

INSPIRING

- Whom do we bring to the exploration of new environments?
- How do we structure interactions among employees with diverse backgrounds?
- How do we structure interactions with interesting outsiders?
- Do we create special settings to stimulate creativity?
- Does our vision inspire people to create and change the world?
- How many resources do we give our people to experiment?
- Do our values encourage chasing breakthrough ideas?
- How do we set the boundaries for people to experiment?
- What is the balance between freedom and boundaries?

nal sources of inspiration to a larger extent, while lower-cost companies set narrower boundaries on their designers. As in any industry, each company manages its creativity in relation to its position in the market.

STAGE TWO: ATTRACT

Startups that believe they have a winning value proposition must entice employees and partners to support them. They need to attract resources to their ideas. Established companies largely face the opposite challenge: they often have plenty of resources, but need to attract and develop new ideas. Much as researchers at universities collaborate with one another to advance their ideas, established companies require new ideas to further develop their solutions. The concept of open innovation captures the fact that complex innovation efforts should build out of internal as well as external ideas.

Citigroup, for example, opened an office in Silicon Valley with venture investing capabilities. Citi Ventures—whose objective is to be near innovation happening in the Valley—invests in startups with new perspectives on banking and exposes the group to these ideas. Philips is another organization looking outside itself for inspiration. Philips's oil-less cooking machine—which fries food using less than one-tenth the oil of conventional fryers—came from an idea that the company picked up in Asia; after acquiring the idea, Philips leveraged its own marketing, sales, and distribution power to grow the business.

S trategic discoveries combine internal and external ideas and resources; thus established companies benefit from designing ways to attract them.

The rapid growth of knowledge across the world means that hundreds of social microsystems now nurture people with both outstanding ideas and the education to develop them. Innovation hubs—where breakthrough startups thrive amid a vibrant ecosystem of ideas—now exist in different regions throughout the world. Innovation requires the Startup Corporation to engage these hubs with the challenge of leveraging their diversity.

Ecosystem Investing

Ecosystem investing captures the idea of established companies immersing themselves in innovation hubs—investing in startups, collaborating with universities, engaging with partners, and attracting interesting people to their networks. It is often implemented by having specific groups within an established organization scout hubs to identify potential sources of ideas. Intel

Venture Capital, the venture arm of Intel, has been investing in startup companies that could not only add to Intel but also increase the use of Intel products. This kind of collaboration often includes taking an equity position, licensing technology both ways, and integrating products from the larger ecosystem into the product offerings of the established player. Johnson and Johnson has integrated more than a dozen drugs through investing and collaborating with startups and research organizations—growing business by commercializing drugs at a fraction of what it usually costs to develop them.[11]

Global innovation often emerges from regional innovation systems—geographies with a concentration of knowledge and dynamism in a particular industry or sector. These systems usually contain a university, but they are also enriched by the presence of startups, research centers, and established companies, which create networks that further advance the region as a knowledge hub. The presence of a few regional innovation systems for different technologies has led large companies to distribute research efforts across the relevant regions for their particular industry. IBM, for example, has eight research laboratories in as many regions—each of which the company deems a knowledge hub. Others such as Alcoa, Procter and Gamble, and General Mills have a director of external innovation to improve the integration with their networks.[12]

Acquisitions

Cisco, the global networking equipment company, based its growth during the first decade of the twenty-first century on acquiring startup companies—making as many as twenty-three acquisitions in one year. A model like this is feasible only if a company is deeply embedded in its environment, both scouting for relevant technologies and acting as a magnet for startups. The company acquired startups with features that advanced the company's current communication solutions as a strategy to feed its own innovation efforts. Internal R&D has supported and integrated these acquisitions, balancing the capabilities that the company has built in the industry with the ability of entrepreneurs to find new products to enhance telecommunications. Cisco relies on balancing market forces with company strengths to guide their acquisition of startups that provide the best value for the solution that Cisco offers its markets.

Acquisitions are used as a mechanism to bring ideas into established companies, but the quality of this mechanism often depends on the quality of the business development department. Access to a rich pipeline, the use of corporate venture capital to collaborate with venture capitalists, and the ability to negotiate and integrate acquisitions all affect a company's ability to attract interesting outside ideas.

QUESTIONS FOR ACTION

ATTRACTING

- How do we generate a rich pipeline of ideas?

- How do we make sure the pipeline is coming from a diverse set of innovators?

- Where are relevant innovation hubs? Where should we be located?

- How do we evaluate potential acquisitions, partnerships, and collaborations?

- How do we integrate the ideas into the innovation process of the company?

STAGE THREE: COMBINE

In contrast to startups, established companies use the pipeline of ideas—from ideas in early development to the acquisition of companies with a more established model—to make combinations that appeal to a larger market. For example, pharmaceutical companies such as Roche are pursuing the potentially very important field of personalized medicine. Adapting diagnostics and therapies to individuals based on personal history and individual genome requires the combination of many technologies and market players—not only people in scientific discovery but also those in areas such as data management, care delivery, and prevention policies. Roche's collaboration with and acquisition of Genentech is part of its effort to combine different approaches to this new concept of medicine.

Combining for Strategic Discoveries

Imagination and inspiration can help us "see" combinations of existing insights that had never been there before. For example, Seoul's subway combined the observation of people waiting at the station with their shopping needs to create virtual stores—walls with screens where commuters can shop while they wait for a train, using their mobile phones to scan the items they want delivered to their homes.

Combination is a fundamental step toward strategic discoveries. Some companies, such as Kennametal, a $3 billion tool manufacturer, set up teams to systematically search for radical ideas. At Kennametal, the innovation group combines insights from design thinking—observations of customers' behaviors and needs—with insights from other aspects of the business model. Logitech, a computer peripherals company, integrates radical ideas into its strategic planning process. Some of these ideas (like the i/o pen) leverage existing resources, structures, and knowledge to bring a radical innovation to market. Others (like wireless technology for peripherals) provide an important competitive advantage to the entire product range of the company. The company also has a process for employees to convey radical ideas to top management and for top management to give them funding and support. Regardless of the method of cross-pollination, the guiding principle of combining is to bring together different perspectives to develop something new.[13]

Systemwide Solutions: The Advantage of Established Companies

Established companies have an advantage in their ability to combine partial solutions into larger, systemwide solutions. For example, renewable energy companies such as Suzlon Energy in India are integrating pieces of the complex energy industry to create end-to-end solutions. They have moved from turbine manufacturing to integrating grid connections, wind mapping, and land sourcing.[14]

Corporate venture capital and business development divisions can scout the environment to find innovations that are at the fringes today, but may be important elements of future business. For instance, BMW's corporate venture arm has invested in MyCityWay, a startup that maps cities for pedestrians and public transportation users; Best Buy's venture group has invested in startups ranging from sleep-tracking gadgets to electric-vehicle charging stations; the venture division of General Mills has invested in startups exploring customer feedback software, social media, and gaming.[15] Yet these departments need to be integrated with the rest of the company so that ideas can be effectively combined with current resources.

QUESTIONS FOR ACTION

COMBINING

- How do we combine different ideas and perspectives to address larger challenges?

- How can ideas, from either outside or inside, leverage our capabilities?

- How does our top management support radical ideas?

- How do we leverage outside ideas to nurture radical innovation?

STAGE FOUR: LEARN

Thomas Edison believed that the most important application of his new gramophone would be recording people's wills. The early users of telegraphs played chess over the wires because nobody had figured out what to do with this technology. Going forward, we will face the same sorts of discovery processes and periods of near-sightedness as we figure out how to apply nano-robotics to preventive health care, or how to adapt our social structures as medical breakthroughs continue to raise life expectancy. Breakthrough innovation is a process of constant discovery.

Strategic discoveries depend on experiments to discover how solutions will work. Innovators need time and resources to learn what works and what doesn't.

Edison once said, "I have not failed. I've simply found ten thousand ways that do not work." Experimenting is about learning. It is far less about whether a particular experiment failed or succeeded than it is about what we can learn from the results. Steve Jobs included saying no to one thousand things as part of innovation. Breakthrough innovation within established companies needs an incubation period to experiment with different models. Such exploration requires both time and resources. Sometimes, exploration can happen under the radar, where business units support but do not interfere with it.

Alternatively, early phases of exploration can happen within controlled environments, and experiments can craft an idea over time. For example, when Google began its development of the Android operating system, the manager in charge of the newly created division was given leeway to shape the effort any way he wanted, from freedom in hiring to shaping the landscape around the building. The objective was so unique and different from other parts of Google that it needed to have its own environment. He had access to almost unlimited resources and no financial objectives in the traditional sense of revenue goals. The team worked together with engineers from partners such as Motorola, Samsung, and HTC.[16] The seed of Android itself was a small startup that Google had acquired. The product went through many alpha and beta releases, and it took the Android team three years before it had a product ready for market release.

Learning requires resources, broad and inspiring goals, and management support. The discovery process is filled with failures and assumptions that turn out to be wrong. Nespresso's business model failed a few times before it found a formula that worked. The original market was restaurants and hotels, but efforts in this direction proved fruitless. Offices were the next target, which also proved to be wrong. It was only when home customers were targeted with a luxury positioning that an effective business model came together.

A breakthrough innovation does not just happen, and sometimes its best application is not immediately evident. Few original ideas are perfect at inception, and most require experimentation to succeed. Again, take Nespresso as an example. The technology Nespresso uses dates back to the 1960s. For about ten years, engineers at Nestlé tweaked and honed the technology until it made great coffee. From there, it took another ten years to develop the business model to commercialize the concept of coffee-by-the-cup.

When it comes to learning in the Startup Corporation, the goal is to try as many ideas as possible, inside the organization as well as outside, at the lowest possible cost. For example, at Whirlpool, employees with promising ideas develop a business case and can get close to $30,000 to complete a proof-of-concept within a hundred-day window. Employees are trained to experiment quickly and cheaply, as startups do in a lean environment. The million-dollar investments into these potentially breakthrough ideas come only after the company has supported learning and experimentation.[17]

Breakthrough innovation hinges on discovery, a fact that is reflected in its inherent risks. Technologies are sometimes ignored for years before a business model that can leverage them effectively is discovered. Businesses that end up disrupting existing markets go through a learning period where the business model is crafted as the company experiments, discovers, and shapes its future to its findings.

QUESTIONS FOR ACTION

LEARNING

- Have we created a unique environment for experimenting with breakthrough innovations?

- How can we experiment quickly and cheaply?

- Does the learning stage have enough resources, freedom, and support to flourish?

- Are the goals at the learning stage broad and visionary rather than narrow and operational?

- Do we perceive failure as a fundamental aspect of learning?

STAGE FIVE: LEVERAGE

A significant advantage that established companies have over startups is their ability to mobilize and scale innovations quickly across markets. Access to global networks and resources makes large companies distinctive in their ability to experiment across different geographies and transfer ideas and innovations around the world. Innovating frugally to create affordable yet high-quality products is a case in point. Walmart is bringing what it has learned about mobile banking from emerging economies to the United States, where about 60 million Americans are either marginally part of, or totally out of the banking system.[18]

Reverse Innovation and Frugal Innovation

Companies such as General Electric and Philips are using their global presence to tap into the creativity of people in emerging markets. Reverse innovation and frugal innovation both emphasize affordability over cutting-edge performance to define newness.

Reverse innovation occurs when products and business models designed for emerging regions make their way into more developed economies. In other words, some products that are first developed for emerging markets are being incorporated as entry-level products in mature markets. This approach contrasts with the traditional approach, in which old designs of products made for mature markets are adapted to fit the needs of emerging economies.

General Electric, for example, designed a low-cost portable electrocardiogram and low-cost portable ultrasound machine for use in rural regions in Asia. The development priorities for these products were cost, ease of use, and portability, followed finally by performance. Both products were developed for emerging markets, and both have been important growth engines for General Electric in these markets. Yet both of them are now also commercialized in the United States for market segments where portability is important—such as emergency crews at the scene of an automobile accident.[19] The US versions of these products—originally developed for Indian and Chinese doctors—retail at an 80 percent markdown from comparable products in the market.

Nokia's 1100 mobile phone, priced at $15, was designed with frugal innovation—innovation where cost is the number-one priority. The phone includes the basic features of a phone: making and receiving calls and texting. It has only one non-critical feature—a small flashlight, popular because of the frequent blackouts in some emerging regions—and it has a nonslip coating to

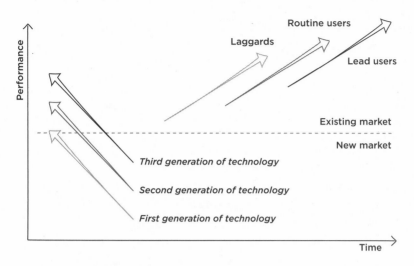

Figure 4.4. The reverse logic of frugal innovation

keep it from slipping in high humidity regions in India.[20] Putting affordability above all other factors can lead to new and exciting products and is an alternative approach to innovation that concentrates on creating superior product performance and quality rather than affordability (figure 4.4).[21]

The Ability to Scale

Dispersed R&D and marketing capabilities allow global players to develop products and services with a worldwide appeal. Companies such as Intel, AstraZeneca, and General Electric all have research centers across the world. Whether research centers are in Germany, India, Israel, or China, each contributes its own expertise, and each contributes local perspectives on the design of new products and services. These companies leverage communication, collaboration, and training software to integrate perspectives that had traditionally been isolated.

When established companies go after the same innovations that startups are pursuing, they often find themselves behind because of the nimble nature of startups. Where these companies have an advantage is in areas that require a combination of different resources and knowledge. Breakthrough innovation from startups can be integrated through acquisitions as part of larger innovations, or the resources of an established company can be used to scale up quickly.

Logitech's acquisition of a startup with a unique technology for remote controls highlights the scaling advantage. While the startup by itself would have faced a complex challenge to convince retailers to stock their product, Logitech was able to integrate the breakthrough technology and take advantage of its own established relationships with retailers around the world. With Logitech behind it, the new device captured a leadership position in the market (with more than one third of market share) in less than a year—ahead of competitors like Sony and Philips. The technology was great, but the startup simply would not have scaled up as quickly as—or without—an existing company.

S trategic discoveries will work best when they are part of complex innovations that leverage the advantages of established companies with access to knowledge, resources, and networks.

Breakthrough innovations with more complex business models—the kind that bring together many different capabilities—are the terrain of established companies. Startups often cannot execute on complex business models because they have limited resources and limited reach. The iPod and iTunes illustrate this complexity. Apple had to develop a piece of hardware, commercialize it globally, convince the music industry to make songs available individually (instead of as albums) for 99 cents, aggregate enough songs to make the service attractive for customers, and still get millions of customers to buy the device and use the service. The resources of established organizations are invaluable when it comes to developing complex solutions such as these.

LEVERAGING

- Does my company go after more complex innovations that leverage its capabilities and knowledge?

- Is my organization trying to replicate innovations that startups do better than established companies?

- Does my company scan startups to identify innovations that will scale much faster through established business models?

- Does my company scan startups to identify innovations that will contribute to more complex innovations through acquisitions or as part of the ecosystem?

STAGE SIX: INTEGRATE

In contrast to the incremental innovation that naturally occurs within a business unit, strategic discoveries often do not have an obvious place to grow and mature within an organization. Breakthrough innovations in the Startup Corporation often face the same challenges as the integration of acquired companies. Nespresso evolved into a separate division within Nestlé; the remote control at Logitech became a separate product, but one that was integrated into the existing structure of the company.

Breakthrough innovations that lead to the creation of a new market may consolidate divisions or, in some cases, take over an existing one. For example, the transition from traditional incandescent lights to LEDs (light-emitting diodes) at Philips moved through various stages. LEDs began as an idea separate from the lighting division—which did not consider LED a legitimate lighting technology—and finished as the division's core technology.

Integration requires an innovation to be mature enough to compete with existing business models. While companies such as Cisco have mastered the process of integrating acquisitions, other companies have become known for their inability to integrate new ideas and transform them to fit existing businesses. The best way to fail at integration is to impose short-term targets on new businesses that are as demanding as those of mature ones. Failure to meet these targets is then often used as an excuse to shift funds away from the acquisition and let it starve until it ultimately becomes irrelevant.

Another way to fail at integration is to use a new product or service to lure customers into old products or services. A company in the enterprise software business struggled to transition from the old implementation-on-site model to a cloud-based model. The company created a new division to adapt to the new cloud-computing model, but when new customers signed up for a 30-day free trial, they would receive a phone call from the implementation side of the company trying to lure them into the older installation model.

Integration must balance the risk of being too early (and allowing business units to focus on efficiency to kill an innovation) with the risk of being too late (and missing out on the opportunity to leverage resources, networks, and knowledge in the company). Successful integration depends very much on the leader of the innovation, his or her credibility within the larger company, and on the support of top management.

The Startup Corporation is in a unique position—able both to exploit its existing resources and market position and to explore new technologies and acquisitions. While each of these stages is important to innovation within the Startup Corporation, their implementation is as varied as the number of companies. Different ideas and circumstances require different solutions.

QUESTIONS FOR ACTION

INTEGRATING

- What has been our success rate of integrating acquired companies?

- How have strategic discoveries performed once they have been integrated into an existing business unit or as a separate one?

- How do we support strategic discoveries as they are integrated into the company as a business on their own?

- How are resources allocated as strategic discoveries become a business on their own?

Implementing the Startup Corporation

5.

THE STARTUP CORPORATION does not have one set design, and its structure does not necessarily mimic that of a startup. While in some cases it does look like a traditional startup—such as Medwinds and Android when they began—often multiple connections to the network of the parent company exist behind the scenes. Each design is adapted to the innovation strategy, industry, resources, and size of its company. Every Startup Corporation is a unique combination of management solutions with a different emphasis on market (external) forces, company (internal) forces, open networks, and internal resources.

From an emotional perspective, the front end of the breakthrough innovation process—inspiring, attracting, combining, and learning—is often the hardest part of pursuing strategic discoveries (figure 5.1). Front-end activities focus on managing early efforts to stimulate creativity, experiment, and learn about which designs are scalable. Most ideas do not become scalable businesses. In some cases, innovations end up being incremental, adding significant value to a company but not moving it into a novel business model. Breakthrough innovation is unpredictable, and the much more common incremental innovation frequently

INSPIRE ATTRACT COMBINE LEARN	LEVERAGE INTEGRATE
Front end	**Back end**

Figure 5.1. Activities of breakthrough innovation

derives from front-end activities. Yet when these early activities are well designed, the chances of crafting a breakthrough are much greater.

Leveraging and integrating, the back-end activities of the breakthrough innovation process necessary to pursue strategic discoveries effectively, tend to be overlooked. Managers get so excited about a unique idea or its potential to create new markets that they forget about the execution side, believing that a great prototype will lead to a great business. Engineers make the same mistake when they trust that a wonderful product will draw customers.

The complexity of breakthrough innovations typically demands significant trial and error to find the correct configuration of a new system. Uncertainty is prevalent, and smart experimentation is the most effective way to gather information. The back-end activities of strategic discoveries require more resources as different system configurations are tested. The later activities also call for a higher level of commitment from various partners, including contracts. In this chapter, we look at possible solutions (or tools, as we also refer to them later) for each activity of the innovation process.

SOLUTIONS FOR INSPIRING

Inspiring sits at the very front of the innovation process. Design thinking and human-centered design have developed numerous techniques to stimulate ideas. These techniques are effective ways for teams to become more creative, whether they are part of an established organization or just beginning with a startup. Table 5.1 outlines three solutions—design units, stealth innovation, and bounded innovation—that focus on taking advantage of

Table 5.1. Solutions for inspiring

Design units	Stealth innovation	Bounded innovation

being part of an established organization. As such, they work along design thinking and human-centered design techniques. While mechanisms may differ, the objective of each is to create new concepts internally—to pursue strategic discoveries using the knowledge and skills that exist within the organization. Yet the inspiration for achieving these objectives still derives from both internal and market forces.

Design Units

Design units are departments fully devoted to creating new ideas. For instance, design units of top-line fashion firms aggressively explore creative concepts, pushing styles that shock the market before being embraced. Designs in clothing, furniture, architecture, and household objects are pure expressions of creativity.[1] They also illustrate how creativity is constructed as a social expression.

Design units generally focus on incremental innovation, developing concepts that are in line with a company's existing strategy. Yet design units can be given the objective to come up with breakthrough ideas. Because such ideas do not simply happen—they are crafted through design cycles—design units need room to explore networks in the business environment and to experiment.

Innovation is, to a large extent, an exercise in copying and combining ideas. While design units pull knowledge from internal resources, they also benefit from studying other industries, utilizing a number of different tools to stimulate innovation (table 5.2).

Import-in innovation. Import-in innovation is about importing ideas from other fields and industries. For instance, electric lightbulbs' screw-like design was based on the design of kerosene lamps. Today, design firms constantly use an import-in innovation approach to transfer ideas from such fields as health care to shoes to distribution and web design.

Design thinking. Design thinking[2] focuses on anthropological techniques to closely observe and question how different people use products, and to identify needs unfulfilled by existing products. For example, a design of the car of the future might start by looking at how kids interact with information technology to inspire new methods of controlling heat, entertainment systems, and safety features. The design unit then goes through stages of divergent and convergent thinking—the push and pull of any design process—to shape these insights into a new product or feature.

Lead-user innovation. Lead-user innovation gets its inspiration from studying advanced users rather than average customers; for example, in the case of bicycles, the focus would be professional cyclists rather than hobbyists.[3] Lead-user innovation builds on the idea that these early users signal what the future of a market will look like.

Table 5.2. Tools to stimulate innovation

Import-in innovation
Design thinking
Lead-user innovation
Value innovation
Future life
Big data

> Design units are teams focused on shaping ideas. They can be structured around a particular stretch goal from top management, or they can be given the objective of creating new concepts.

Value innovation. Value innovation unearths the deeply held assumptions of an industry and then challenges them to create new value propositions; it is an effort to identify new dimensions of value and redefine competition.[4] For instance, Zara challenged the assumption that fashion changed seasonally by churning out new designs year-round; it also challenged the assumption that a particular design would be available throughout the season by not replenishing stock when an item sold out.

Future life. As a strategy, future life examines emerging trends and life structures to project potentially large future markets based on those trends and structures becoming mainstream in ten or more years. Future life, like lead-user innovation, focuses on experts in different fields; it may even go so far as to ask kids how they see the future.

Big data. While statistical analyses do not provide answers per se (correlation is not causation, after all), big data can identify trends that might otherwise remain hidden. Study of such information often leads to incremental ideas for improving existing products, but it can also inspire breakthrough innovations. For example, the casino company Harrah's has used detailed data on its customers to personalize marketing, while web-based companies consistently analyze large amounts of data to infer customer behavior.[5]

Stealth Innovation

Stealth innovation relies on the ingenuity of a company's existing employees. Some complex strategic discoveries are best visualized by a select group that brings together different perspectives.

For centuries, universities have depended upon the inventiveness of their people and their ability to collaborate to come up with breakthrough ideas.

The group working on stealth innovation projects in their initial stages may have little formal structure—there are likely no deadlines, no periodic reviews, no top management attention, and none of the day-to-day pressure typical of business units. If breakthrough ideas are exposed to the larger organization too soon, the ideas will attract criticism before they are strong enough to stand on their own.

In their early phases, stealth innovation projects require time. Companies fully focused on execution, in which people have little time to play with ideas, will hardly benefit from this approach, and that focus is precisely what makes the innovation paradox a reality. If time to explore is not formally available to employees, either people will not experiment at all, or they will do their own curiosity-driven investigation on personal time. For the latter to occur, a strong culture of commitment and rewards needs to exist, which most organizations lack.

Strategic discoveries can happen if people have both the time to network and experiment and the motivation to explore opportunities outside the current strategy.

Exploratory projects also need additional financial support—often a relatively small amount—access to other parts of the organization and the broader organizational network, protection from early scrutiny, and an advocate to build support throughout the organization.[6]

One example of stealth innovation happening within a company is pfizerWorks, a platform that frees up researchers and managers to focus on tasks specific to their specialized skills.

Researchers at Pfizer can use the platform for such tasks as editing an article or expanding a draft presentation into a professional one, saving them precious research time.

The idea for pfizerWorks initially came from an employee who worked on his free time to create the business model. He leveraged his connections with suppliers, and a group of internal people agreed to team up and help him develop the concept. His boss provided resources and access to internal and external networks otherwise not available to him. Various prototypes were tested, and by the time the idea was shared with the larger organization, the concept was operational and debugged enough for people to both use it and easily understand its value.[7]

The principles of stealth innovation are also becoming effective in social innovation. Whereas governments have a history of top-down management and traditionally have been the innovators in social policies, information and communication technology now offer citizens the tools to organize themselves. For instance, networks exist for neighbors to support each other in ways not previously possible. Some allow neighbors to help seniors with their shopping, while others connect older cooks with neighbors who want an authentic food experience as well as a social outlet. Collaboration also enables people to report infrastructure in need of repair to local authorities. Individuals' ability to organize beyond the scope of what governments can do has been proven again and again after catastrophes such as earthquakes and hurricanes. As these initiatives succeed, they spread out to other neighborhoods and cities, improving society without waiting for local authorities to support them.[8]

Bounded Innovation

A third way to inspire internal solutions is bounded innovation. Tata's Nano car and BMVSS's efforts to bring affordable yet functional leg prostheses to India's poor are examples of bounded innovation—innovation that is limited by economic criteria.[9] Bounded innovation, like other solutions for the inspiration activity, can happen as a stand-alone effort that leads to the development of a specific product, or it can target complex systems that require the combination of multiple technologies and networks.

Both frugal innovation and reverse innovation, for example, are approaches we have mentioned in which the vision of a stretch goal from top management inspires people to look for solutions that would have otherwise been ignored. An important principle of each approach is to stimulate creativity to achieve a low overall cost with a high-cost-to-performance ratio. The product itself should also be different enough from existing products to require solutions based on different paradigms.

SOLUTIONS FOR ATTRACTING

Management solutions for attracting ideas and innovations from outside networks include corporate venturing, discovery units, and competitions (table 5.3). These solutions all rely on market forces to a larger extent than do solutions for inspiring.

Corporate Venturing

Large companies have mimicked certain aspects of the startup process, and corporate venture capital (CVC) has been the most common approach. Based on the traditional venture capital model, established companies invest in promising startups and support them through their growth phases.

At first glance, the logic of CVC is straightforward—replicate the venture capital aspect of startups. Yet several critical differences separate the two approaches. Traditional venture capital

Table 5.3. Solutions for attracting

Corporate venturing

Discovery units

Competitions and tournaments

funds have a single objective: to maximize returns for their investors. While this task is not easy (no more than 25 percent of these funds return above their cost of capital), at least the objective is clearly defined. Venture capitalists need to possess a quality network to attract interesting companies, the skills to select those that have the potential to create a new market or disrupt an existing one, and the experience and contacts to help each startup discover the business model that can best realize its growth potential.

Corporate venture capital, on the other hand, has a more complex set of objectives. Although one objective is certainly financial returns, the other objectives are much less tangible. CVC divisions must support the strategy of the company identifying startups that provide technologies to complement the ones the company has, use new technologies that can be incorporated into the company's current business models, and support the broader ecosystem of the company—either by creating markets that will use the company's products or by simplifying access to critical resources. Measuring the return on these nonfinancial objectives is difficult.

Another aspect that differentiates CVC and traditional venture capital is the access to networks that they give startup companies. While top venture capitalists have access to high-quality networks of engineers and managers, service providers, large companies, and bankers—often with startup experience—the advantage of CVC is that it provides startup companies with access to the pool of resources, capabilities, global reach, and markets of a large corporation.

The incentive structure of CVC and traditional venture capital is another point of distinction.[10] Traditional venture capital has a clear reward structure—one that takes advantage of having a single, measurable objective. The basic pillars include a small management fee (1 or 2 percent of funds under management) and a large success fee (up to 30 percent of returns). CVC incentive structure is more complicated, as are the setting and evaluation of objectives. CVC managers also tend to be more risk-averse than their independent counterparts because failure in the corporate world can be much more expensive from a personal perspective. This risk aversion often leads to CVC investing in less innovative projects—to both reduce risks and ease the integration into existing businesses.

Often CVC divisions have offices in entrepreneurial hot spots, such as Silicon Valley for IT, San Diego for biotech, London and New York for entertainment, and Beijing for China business models. Maintaining offices in regions where entrepreneurial innovation is happening gives CVC quick access to radical ideas.

Corporate venture capital attracts radical ideas and takes equity positions in startups. It can be an effective way for early access to external hubs of innovation.

The initial commitment of CVC frequently is financial—taking an equity position in the startup company. CVC divisions rely on market forces in entrepreneurial regions to select their investments. Investment decisions hinge on consensus among venture capitalists as to the overall value of a startup, while corporate considerations act as boundaries for identifying potential candidates. For investments in early rounds, CVC delegates the management of the startup to agents in the local ecosystem. Only when the startup has crafted a high-growth business model does CVC broker agreements between the startup and the large company to ultimately leverage the assets of the company to accelerate startup growth.

As CVC moves from market forces to organization forces to deliver on breakthrough innovation, the challenge becomes brokering between startups and different departments in the corporation.

Discovery Units

Discovery units involve corporate efforts that focus on partnering with open networks to identify breakthrough opportunities. Discovery units are often part of the innovation department, integrated either as business development or as corporate venturing. In contrast to design units, which work on fostering ideas within the company, discovery units focus on attracting ideas from the open network. Established companies can outsource selection of promising startups to market forces and then integrate products as winners emerge. Discovery units fulfill the role of scouting the market for potentially game-changing ideas.

Discovery units are based on the belief that more ideas happen outside the company than inside (again, it's simply the law of large numbers), and selection forces—whether within the market or within the academic institution—do a good job of sorting out the likely winners. For example, companies like General Mills and Procter and Gamble have teamed up with a crowd-funding site, CircleUp Network, to track which startups in the consumer goods field are getting funded.[11] Discovery units recognize that established companies are not the best at coming up with breakthrough ideas, but they do have the necessary networks and resources to scale them up quickly. Established companies can be dangerous fast seconds that simply scale faster than the initial innovators.[12]

Large companies have discovery units and mergers and acquisitions (M&A) departments to identify ideas that market forces have already filtered, and to integrate them into the company. This outsourcing of the early activities of the innovation process is fully consistent with open innovation concepts and, more importantly, is often a more efficient approach to innovation.

While discovery units focus much of their effort on integrating products into existing businesses (reflecting the fact that incremental innovation consumes the lion's share of innovation budgets), they can also be used to create the ecosystem required to devise breakthrough innovation solutions. Startup corporations are best at creating complex solutions, and acquisitions and external ideas are often important parts of these solutions.

Innovation cells are an alternative to discovery units; these cells team up with universities and research centers to transfer technology. Innovation cells are designed to take advantage of scientific progress and its translation into new technologies. These activities often happen in top universities and research centers, frequently with financial support from governments. Yet governments are now demanding closer links between universities and businesses. Part of this effort is to ease the legal requirements for transferring technology out of universities, while another aspect is to encourage universities to transfer their knowledge.

Innovation cells rely on the university environment to stimulate the discovery and development of breakthrough technologies, and the École Politechnique Fédérale de Lausanne (EPFL) is one of the universities where companies have located innovation cells. Founded in 1853, EPFL generates about fifteen startups, forty-five patents, and forty-five licenses per year. The university has established different vehicles to link technology and industry, some of which include a technology transfer office, alliances for university-industry joint research, support for startup companies, and a team that looks for market applications of new technologies. These efforts are integrated physically in the Innovation Square, a campus that houses more than one hundred startups, as well as twelve cells from companies such as Cisco, Logitech, Nestlé, Credit Suisse, and Constellium.

D iscovery units scout the environment to access opportunities that market forces have already worked on. They focus on startup companies and research organizations that are often the source of breakthrough ideas. Alternatively, innovation cells team up with universities and research centers to transfer technology.

People in innovation cells are in constant touch with technology-based startups, exposed to ideas from other industries, and encouraged to join projects. The social infrastructure is set to create the informal relationships that spark collaboration. Innovation cells also encourage exchanges between researchers at various levels and employees at companies that license the technologies and bring them to market. For example, Philips has transformed its central R&D facility in the Netherlands into a hub that brings together more than a dozen companies that interact among themselves as well as with Philips—planting the seeds of innovation in vibrant soil.

Competitions and Tournaments

Innovation tournaments rely on competition as a powerful way to stimulate both effort and creativity. Sports are grounded in a competitive spirit, athletes exert their maximum effort, and teams invent imaginative tactics to beat their opponents. Amateur players engage in sports for the thrill of participating and winning, but professional sports add important economic incentives. Similar forces are used in business and innovation management.

In innovation tournaments (also referred to as innovation contests, technology contests, or tournaments for ideas), people compete to win a prize. Tournament designs vary; some are suited to encourage incremental ideas, while others spur radical ones. For instance, a large multinational company in data management runs an internal, multiple-round innovation competition every year. Within each business unit, projects compete and a winner is selected. All the unit winners participate in a final round at headquarters, and three winners are chosen out of ten finalists. The winners receive a few thousand dollars, as well as funding to pursue their idea. The structure of this kind of competition—internal, with rounds at the business-unit level, three prizes, and a relatively small reward—is designed to deliver incremental ideas.

An example of a tournament for fostering breakthrough ideas was the Ansari X Prize, used to develop space tourism solutions

Innovation tournaments are powerful tools that involve a large number of people in generating ideas. Breakthrough innovation and incremental innovation require different tournament design.

for a new market, with technologies that had not been combined before. The competition was open to the public, but, because of the size of the investment, the actual number of groups was limited. The prize was $10 million for the first group to launch a reusable, manned aircraft into space twice in fifteen days. However, the winner—the Tier One project backed by Microsoft cofounder Paul Allen—actually spent more than $100 million to meet the challenge.

Innovation design decisions define the structure of the competition and the rules for choosing winners. Clear and fair rules with neutral judges help encourage an attitude and perception of fairness that can attract more competitors. Judges may be experts or they may be chosen from the public or peer groups. Smaller, more numerous prizes, various rounds, and presentations with other teams, including cross-pollinating ideas, emphasize cooperation. Such a design reinforces knowledge sharing and collaboration, which, while not bad in and of themselves, are more conducive for developing incremental innovation. Innovation tournaments are best suited for breakthroughs when groups compete against each other in few rounds with a winner-takes-all prize. Table 5.4 outlines the characteristics of innovation tournaments for encouraging different types of innovation.

The Internet has made it possible to reach large numbers of people from around the world in open tournaments. Platforms such as Innocentive, an e-business incubated at Eli Lilly that was subsequently spun off, allow companies to post different problems, with responses ranging from brainstorms to ideas requiring transfer of intellectual property to concepts that lead

Table 5.4. Structures of innovation tournaments

DESIGN DECISIONS	INCREMENTAL INNOVATION	BREAKTHROUGH INNOVATION
Population	Internal employees	Open to the public
Group size	Unlimited	Limited
Prize	Several prizes	Winner takes all
Size of reward	Small	Large
Rounds	Several	Few
Participants	Many—wisdom of crowds	Few—wisdom of experts
Goals	Specific	Broad
Stages	Few	Multiple
Collaboration	Group presentations	Interim milestones
Occurrence	Recurring	One-time
Feedback	Frequent and open to other players	Limited

to collaboration between the company and the winner. These platforms provide neutral grounds for tournaments and usually employ a winner-takes-all structure, with prizes that can reach $1 million. The contests identify not only great solutions to problems but also great talent.

Innovation tournaments, based on competition, reproduce an important part of the startup environment. They are best suited to the early stages of the innovation process—and only if problems are precisely defined. As problems become broader, discovery and execution become more relevant.

SOLUTIONS FOR COMBINING

Corporate venturing bridges the activities of attracting and combining in the process of pursuing breakthrough innovation. Acquisitions are intended to both attract interesting innovations into the company and combine them with an existing business unit or larger breakthrough innovation effort. Whereas collaboration involves coordinating partnerships and networks to address complex challenges, incubators within established companies are an alternative solution to combining ideas (table 5.5).

Incubators and Accelerators

The original incubators were independent entities to support entrepreneurs in their initial stages of development, and the concept has been around for several decades. Through incubators, entrepreneurs can move faster, and with better knowledge of whether their business idea is feasible. In addition to providing services such as legal support and accounting, incubators give entrepreneurs access to business angels, venture capitalists, communications, marketing, and international networks. Whereas incubators play a nurturing role, accelerators take a heavier hand, supplying money and mentorship for short periods—sometimes as little as three months—to validate, pivot, or shut down the startup.

Governments have used incubators to demonstrate their commitment to entrepreneurship, and to innovation as a growth engine for the local economy. These publicly funded efforts often do not require anything from startups (other than participation once selected, of course). Private incubators, in contrast, frequently demand resources from the startup in exchange for

Table 5.5. Solutions for combining

Incubators and accelerators
Collaboration
Corporate venturing

support. Such resources range from rent to the more common equity participation.

Established companies have picked up on the concept of incubators, and many have translated it into internal efforts that support breakthrough innovation. The principle of corporate incubators is similar to that of private incubators—both provide support during the early stages of an idea. Corporate incubators focus on intrapreneurs, company employees who have an idea worth exploring further. The incubator offers them company resources, access to internal talent and knowledge, and time and money. The incubator also protects these radical innovators from the short-term focus of business units.

Incubators provide an environment designed to support the unique needs of strategic discoveries in the early phases. Accelerators adapt this environment to later stages when the discovery process is closer to the market.

Corporate incubators or accelerators also house entrepreneurs with startups relevant to the larger ecosystem of the corporation. Philips has launched more than two dozen ventures using the incubator model, and its management views incubation as an effective way to transform ideas into potential businesses. Incubation gives Philips the opportunity to further leverage its R&D efforts.[13] Misys—a London-based software firm with customers in financial services and health-care industries—is another example. To leverage open-source technology, it created a separate unit to house projects with ideas for both markets, eventually developing products that won contracts when competing against the original health-care division.[14]

Collaboration

The Smart car was a result of the partnership between Daimler–Benz (Mercedes) and the Swatch Group, the Swiss leader in watches. The idea was to create a new car category for urban needs, merging the technical automobile knowledge of Daimler–Benz and the design skills of Swatch. The concept was not an instant success, as is the case with many radical concepts. Introduced in 1998, it took more than a decade to gain the success it now has. The factory in Hambach, France, is now running at capacity, as customers grasp the benefits of the Smart proposition— likely helped along by rising fuel prices. The innovative item is the outcome of bringing together two very different views on cars, design, and the future of urban mobility.[15]

Partnerships and coordinating innovation networks are other ways companies can approach combination. Startup corporations create solutions rather than individual products, and these strategic discoveries often require the collaboration of a number of parties beyond the original company. The idea of collaboration shares some of the ideas of open innovation and co-creation.

Co-creation refers to collaboration with external parties throughout the innovation process. In most cases, co-creation is associated with incremental innovation efforts as a development team incorporates input and design ideas from customers early in the development process. Co-creation mainly relies on the wisdom of crowds, and it is embedded in the larger concept of crowdsourcing. Web communities in which users post evaluations of products, suggesting new features and improvements, are a great source of ideas. Gaming apps, for example, heavily depend on their communities of followers to choose new features for their games. They co-create their games with their communities.

Although if co-creation is more commonly used to develop incremental innovation, it can be applied to breakthrough innovation as well. The race to create a new way to consume television—much like Apple did with the iPod and iTunes for music—is bringing together a variety of partners, each with a piece of the puzzle. Breakthroughs like these are not simply about shaping how new products will look, but how entire new industries will function. Google is collaborating with a number of partners in television—including consumer electronics manufacturers and content providers—and Chromecast is Google's attempt to be the central player in the merging of television and Internet technologies.[16]

Partnerships are an effective way to bring together the disparate knowledge that breakthrough innovations require.

Open-source initiatives are another example of leveraging partnerships for combination. In software, Linux is probably the best-known example of co-creation that led to a radical concept—a free and open operating system. In the pharmaceutical and biotechnology industries, partnerships sharing disparate knowledge in the interest of innovation are common. For instance, Pfizer partners with rivals such as Johnson & Johnson and Elan Pharmaceuticals to bring Alzheimer's drugs to the market. The partnership combines the knowledge of the partners and helps them diversify the risks of innovation investments in the range of $1 billion.[17]

Corporate Venturing Revisited

Corporate venturing can be fruitfully used for combining when its investments are intended to add new products to a larger breakthrough effort. The objective of these investments is to create the ecosystem for a new market. In contrast to corporate venturing in the attracting activity, here the corporate venture capital unit considers combining investments to create a larger breakthrough innovation.

SOLUTIONS FOR LEARNING

The learning activity is arguably the most unique to breakthrough innovation, and its core objective is to discover a winning formula. For breakthrough products and services, establishing an effective business model frequently proves to be the most challenging task. Often, the customer segment that was originally considered to be the best for innovation fails to work, and only after trial and error is the right customer segment discovered. In other cases, the original supply-chain design and suppliers fail to deliver, and a new design is needed. Innovations that create new systems—not simply new products—require more complex business models. Discovering customers, suppliers, and supply chains is one hurdle, but enticing partners and other actors in the market is also challenging.

The learning activity is about discovering the business model that works. It uses experiments to learn and craft the solution that will be scaled up.

The core of the learning activity is designing experiments (including prototypes), learning from them, and adapting the discovery process to the learning that accrues over time (table 5.6). Breakthrough innovation cannot be planned in the same way that incremental innovation can because of the embedded uncertainties, but also because the path forward depends on the experiments' outcomes. Learning is about discovering the business

Table 5.6. Solutions for learning

Incubators and accelerators
Experimenting
Prototyping

model that works by experimenting as cheaply and as quickly as possible. Experiments require knowledge and intuition (both to design them and to interpret the results) and luck. Finding a customer from a segment that was not considered part of the business model, or connecting with a supplier with a compatible set of skills, is all part of this luck. For example, Novartis's Gleevec drug was initially developed to combat a rare blood cancer that strikes a few thousand patients worldwide. After it was developed and in the market, it was also shown to be effective for treating six other diseases; it eventually hit $3.7 billion in sales. Dan Vasella, Novartis's CEO at the time, acknowledged that luck played a role in this growth.[18] While you certainly can't force luck, you can be ready to capitalize on it when it swings in your favor.

Incubators and Accelerators Again

As we described earlier, incubators and accelerators provide a unique environment for facilitating the combination of ideas, but they are helpful as well in structuring the learning activity. "Failure" is seen not as a lack of success but rather as part of the learning process about how to design future experiments. Incubators understand that not meeting initial expectations is an opportunity to learn and adapt before big investments are made. This conception of failure sharply contrasts with that of most business units, in which failing to meet the plan turns on all the alarms. That viewpoint explains why breakthrough innovations within business units often struggle to prosper; missing expectations is a red flag that causes leaders to divest more rapidly than more adventurous business structures might allow.

But incubators and accelerators are not the only structures that aid learning. Useful learning happens with stealth innovation practices, allowing a certain group of individuals to explore and experiment alongside (and unimpeded by) the everyday workings of the organization—if business unit managers support these activities. Discovery can also take place in innovation networks, discovery units, or teams designed to address boundary innovation, as well as with the help of corporate venture capital. Each of these structures helps fulfill the objective of the learning activity as long as experimenting is part of the design.

Experimenting

Discovery planning refers to the experimentation that happens in breakthrough innovation.[19] What makes the concept of discovery planning interesting is its inherent contradiction—a discovery cannot be planned in the way that an incremental improvement can. That said, little "planning" actually occurs in the traditional sense. Of course, designing the next experiment can be considered planning, but the step beyond that is largely unknown; the way forward is informed by the learning acquired through each experiment. Still, each experiment needs to be carefully designed for maximum learning, minimum cost, and sharpest results. The experiment is then painstakingly executed and the learning interpreted. These three steps—design, experiment, and learn—comprise a unit of discovery (figure 5.2).

UNIT OF DISCOVERY

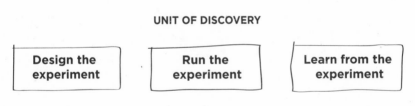

Figure 5.2. Discovery

Several experiments can happen concurrently, as business models have aspects that are not necessarily connected. Tools such as design thinking aid in product or service design, and concepts such as the value chain and the business model canvas[20] help explore the business model design.

Prototyping

Using prototypes to experiment provides significant learning per unit of investment. Internet businesses release beta versions of new products with little marketing effort to keep traffic low but quickly get feedback from customers. Physical products benefit from rapid prototyping techniques that tools such as 3D printers provide. Such prototypes do not need to be fully functional; much testing can be done on a new product's physical appearance. Also, testing a particular feature does not require that other features be operational.

E xperimenting and prototyping are two of the most effective ways to test breakthrough ideas. Careful design and execution will provide the most learning.

Prototyping also extends to the business model, to quickly learn what works and what doesn't. Internet business models are easiest to test. Landing pages' pricing structures differ so companies can learn about customer reaction to varying pricing strategies. Even physical stores can utilize prototypes. For example, Steve Jobs's prototype of the Apple store—a warehouse that was a full-scale, fully stocked store—was ultimately decisive in designing and shaping the overall customer experience.[21]

SOLUTIONS FOR LEVERAGING

The experimentation that occurs during the learning and leveraging activities ultimately leads to execution. The ideal outcome of the learning effort is both a technology model and a business model that are strong enough to be scaled up. Leveraging focuses on building the business's culture, growth path, and management infrastructure (table 5.7). Often, organizations assume that this transformation will happen naturally, but such transitions are difficult and benefit from designing these processes. They are resource intensive, and potential cannibalization or synergies with existing business units happen at this stage.

Table 5.7. Solutions for leveraging

Culture
Growth
Infrastructure

Culture

A business's culture begins to form as soon as two people come together. This foundation can be reshaped effectively as the entrepreneurial team becomes a management team. Some of the early cultural traits will survive long into the life of the business, but during leveraging they need to be consciously shaped. Management highlights experiences during the formation period that best reflect the new business's values. These experiences will become part of the business's mythology and, as with any myth, will epitomize the ways in which the organization is and has remained aligned with its core values.

Each organization has stories and myths that exemplify its values. Siebel Systems, for example, highlighted how Tom Siebel fired one of his best salespeople because the man did not respect the passion for customer service that was a fundamental value of the company. Nespresso's culture reinforces how the business exists because the early team members called every single one of their friends to buy a Nespresso machine—so they would hit the target that Nestlé had given them to stay alive.

Leveraging marks the transition from an entrepreneurial to a managerial perspective. Carefully developed processes can lessen the challenges of this difficult transition.

Growth

Another aspect of leveraging is changing the mentality from a focus on breakthrough, experimentation, and discovery to one in which efficiency, execution, and incremental innovation take the driver's seat. People value the activities and attitudes that have made them successful. Changing to a management approach that may be at odds with the one that has brought them to this point is not easy.

Part of the transformation from an entrepreneurial organization to a functional one is setting the stage to facilitate further growth. At this point, the team has to deploy supply chains, distribution channels, manufacturing operations, and support functions such as marketing. In doing so, the relationship between the experimental elements of the Startup Corporation and the rest of the company shifts toward a broader collaboration. The Startup Corporation team—once isolated from the rest of the company, to prevent early criticism and keep it separate from the everyday workings of the organization—now needs access to a large number of touch points within the company. The speed of growth and the reach of the deployment will depend on the ability to establish and leverage these links.

Infrastructure

A final aspect of the leveraging activity is building management infrastructure. At this point, the Startup Corporation adopts a functional organization, and role descriptions emerge. Standard operating procedures for processes such as measurement systems, planning systems, budgeting, and planning become more formal than before. Establishing a human resource management department marks the official transition to the leveraging activity.

SOLUTIONS FOR INTEGRATING

The final activity for successful breakthrough innovations is integration, for which there are three broad solutions: working the breakthrough into an existing business unit, spinning it off, or keeping it as a separate division (table 5.8).

Table 5.8. Solutions for integrating

Reconfiguration
Spin-off
New division

Reconfiguration

Breakthrough innovations can reconfigure, and sometimes even replace, existing business units. LED lighting, for example, reworked the lighting division of companies such as Philips. The new technology made the old incandescent technology obsolete to most applications, and options for new products and markets further shifted the business unit. This type of integration is difficult. It requires changing the way managers and employees in the division see their business model. The natural reaction to the redefinition of existing business units is to fight the breakthrough innovation in favor of maintaining the status quo.

Certain breakthroughs can be integrated into existing business units. This solution is more common when the breakthrough happens at the product rather than the system level. Pharmaceutical products, for example, can be scientific breakthroughs that create huge new markets, sometimes in the billions of dollars.

Spin-Off

Spin-offs are alternatives for breakthrough innovations that do not fit with a company's corporate strategy. Spin-offs can become independent companies, as did Guidant, Eli Lilly's medical devices division. The division was created out of Eli Lilly's purchase of several startups in the medical devices business. These startups were incubated within the corporation, and while some grew to become large businesses, others failed to build a sustainable competitive advantage. Eli Lilly floated Guidant in the stock market, and before it was later acquired, Guidant had become the second-largest medical devices company in the United States.

New Division

An alternative to spinning off a breakthrough as an independent company is to sell it. Sometimes the new division fits better with another company than with the company that originated it. British Telecom, for example, partners with venture capital firms to sell companies from inside BT. These businesses often offer services that support BT's ecosystem but are not core to the company. To reflect this process, full or partial spin-offs have been labeled as inside-out open innovation.[22]

B reakthrough innovations can be integrated into existing business units, but often they are spun off as separate companies or new business units.

In certain cases, the original company may buy back the piece of equity that it sold when originally spinning off the innovation—most often when the evolution of the stand-alone startup brings it back to the core of the larger company, or when the objective of the initial partial spin-off was to ease financial needs. For instance, Lucent Technologies decided to spin off a digital video project that it considered to be outside its immediate strategy. When the spun-off video technology proved successful in emerging markets (and was often sold together with Lucent products), the fit between both companies' products led Lucent to buy back the spin-off.

An intermediate solution between a spin-off and a separate division is to create a different company in which the corporation maintains a relevant equity position. This solution reflects a tension between the fit within the current corporate strategy and the option to be relevant to future changes in strategy. Nespresso, for example, is now one of the most profitable divisions within Nestlé. The entire process—from the original idea through determining the workable business model to Nespresso's growth as a business beyond the $1 billion mark—happened as a separate unit. Because of Nespresso's unique business model, Nestlé kept it as a separate business even when it reached an adequate size and a maturity to consider integrating it within the coffee division of the corporation.

The activities leading to successful innovation can be messy, especially at the outset, and no two processes of discovery are alike. As many companies as there are, there are innovation journeys. A thorough understanding of innovation processes can help an organization avoid the pitfalls that leave some companies unable to execute on a great idea, and still others incrementally innovating themselves into obsolescence.

QUESTIONS FOR ACTION

INSPIRING

- What tools does my organization have in place to inspire and stimulate people?

- How does my organization look at other industries to get ideas?

- How much time does my organization devote to bringing together different perspectives and new experiences?

- What are the main sources of inspiration and creativity within my organization?

ATTRACTING

- What tools does my organization use to integrate itself into innovative environments?

- Does my organization get involved in startups that can be relevant to its future?

- Does my organization collaborate with research institutions?

- Does my organization use tournaments to attract ideas?

QUESTIONS FOR ACTION

COMBINING

- How does my company support the initial exploration of ideas?

- Does my organization use incubators to support the initial exploration of ideas?

- How does my company work with external partners to investigate new ideas?

- Does my company invest in promising startups or venture capital funds as a way to access new ideas?

LEARNING

- How does my company design experiments to learn about a potential innovation?

- How does my company use prototyping to learn?

- How is the planning of experiments integrated into innovation development at my company?

LEVERAGING

- What is the process in my organization to move from discovery to integration?

- What tools are in place to ease the scaling up of innovations?

- How does my organization integrate innovation groups with existing businesses?

INTEGRATING

- What alternatives can my organization use to capture the value of breakthrough innovation?

- How hard is it in my organization to create a separate business unit or spin off a new division?

6.
Overcoming the Innovation Paradox
Designing the Startup Corporation

THE PREVIOUS CHAPTERS looked at the various causes of the innovation paradox, as well as why the Startup Corporation can be beneficial for leveraging the resources of established companies toward breakthrough innovations. We have also examined a number of solutions that organizations can implement to better pursue breakthrough innovation. This chapter explores different ways of combining these solutions, depending on the characteristics of the company.

Breakthrough innovation is both risky and difficult. More often than not, the resources that are supposed to go into strategic discoveries end up supporting an incremental innovation or a new product platform for an existing business. In other cases, valuable time and resources get expended on apparently useless efforts, resulting in very little to show in terms of concrete innovations. However, the fact that an endeavor falls short or becomes a new technology for an existing business is not a sign of failure; it is simply part of the game. Strategic discoveries are rare, and they do not happen overnight. They are frequently the outcome of sustained efforts smartly deployed. Apparent failures can turn out to be great businesses as people return to old experiments and build them into new solutions.

This is what makes the innovation paradox so counterintuitive. The elements that allow established companies to scale up keep them from developing breakthrough innovations. On the opposite side of the same coin, the greatest ideas are little more than smoke without the ability and resources to execute. Successful organizations can't simply sit back on their haunches when their current business models are succeeding; neither can those with breakthrough ideas bank on their wits alone. To overcome the innovation paradox, the Startup Corporation takes advantage of established companies' unique set of capabilities to address complex innovations, bringing together disparate technologies and partners to create a new market or industry. It also overcomes the innovation paradox by allowing established companies to avoid the creative roadblocks of routinized processes and leverage their resources to scale up when breakthroughs do occur.

The design of this kind of innovation effort relies on:

1. following a structured process that gives both direction and boundaries as well as the freedom to go back and forth as the solution is crafted
2. management solutions that combine market and company forces in different ways and at different stages of the innovation process
3. combining internal resources with access to rich networks

MANAGING BREAKTHROUGH INNOVATION PROJECTS

Breakthrough innovation is about managing ignorance. The vision of arriving at a strategic discovery is inspiring, but it almost never provides a map of how to get there. The management of breakthrough innovations cannot rely on existing knowledge, because oftentimes there is none. There are no visible milestones, and visualizing the future is hard. Breakthrough innovations require a frame of mind different from that of typical business units.

Managing inspiration stimulates creativity in various ways. It exposes employees to new ideas and environments—having them visit customers, distributors, and trade shows throughout the world. Such journeys can bring together cross-functional teams made up of people with different perspectives and create trust across an organization. These teams also forge ties between technology and markets, creating working groups of engineers and marketing people.

In addition to inspiring their own employees, companies successful at fostering breakthroughs often have a department dedicated to attracting noteworthy startups. When an idea is deemed interesting enough to be evaluated, the team presents it to top management. To ensure that breakthrough innovation ideas do not compete against incremental ideas that nurture existing businesses, top management may have a budget earmarked for breakthrough innovations.

If top management sees that an idea has potential, it gets an initial allocation of hours for chosen team members—anywhere from 20 to 80 percent of their time—as well as money. With these resources, team members further explore technology and possible customers. Once the team needs additional resources, it goes back to top management armed with fresh knowledge. The project is then evaluated based on the new information the team has generated. At that point, a decision is made to either kill the project or provide it with further funding. This determi-

---

B reakthrough innovation is the combination of six activities, and all of them need to be managed. Excelling at some but failing at others will get you only partway.

---

nation always involves top management but may include industry experts and venture capitalists as well. "Go/no go" decisions are based not on milestones and quantitative information, but rather on the business's overall potential. The process progresses through various rounds until either uncertainties are low enough for executing a clear business model or the project is scrapped.

Even when an innovation reaches the market, work still needs to be done to fully realize an effective business model. Often the initial business model lacks strength, and the original customer segment is not as interested as anticipated. Nespresso targeted hotels, restaurants, and offices before a new manager figured out they should target end customers with a premium price product. The i/o pen from Logitech attempted the retail market before it became apparent that a business-to-business model was more adequate. The Silicon Valley–based startup specializing in supply-chain software (presented in chapter 3) went after small and medium enterprises (SMEs) before serendipitously discovering that large companies were a much better target.

As innovations move through the innovation process, challenges become greater. Scaling up is often much harder than coming up with an idea. Even so, most efforts at companies, nonprofits such as business schools, and governments focus on idea generation rather than scaling up. Combining and learning are more difficult than inspiring and attracting ideas. Leveraging and integrating provoke companies, especially when existing businesses view innovations as threats to their own success.

INSPIRING THE STARTUP CORPORATION

Successful management of strategic discoveries depends on managing the portfolio of mechanisms that shape the Startup Corporation—inspiring, attracting, combining, learning, leveraging, and integrating. A company with well-designed foundations that understands the specific needs of breakthrough innovation can better move to structure this portfolio. Without the right foundations, implementation is bound to fail.

The inspiration phase is mostly an internal process; it stimulates the creativity of employees and their networks. Design units, stealth innovation, and bounded innovation each use different techniques to elicit and support internal inventiveness. All heavily depend on interacting with the business environment, but they ultimately place their trust in employees to discover radical ideas. Companies that have hired and developed passionate people and have created a risk-taking, trustworthy organization can best leverage these techniques. These organizational designs protect people from market and company forces that identify the still-weak aspects of a concept, while downplaying its potential before it is fully developed. They provide resources for experimentation, as well as encourage stimulation through interactions with open networks.

Design units bring people with different backgrounds together around the shared objective of coming up with strategic discoveries. Access to resources and an experimental approach support this structure. Sources of inspiration range from ethnographic approaches for discovering customers' needs to data mining, to uncover hidden behaviors.

Stealth innovation relies on the organization giving some employees—usually those involved in technology and markets, but in certain cases people in other functions—room to experiment. In the early stages of a strategic discovery, ideas are often imported and adapted from other industries. This process is open in the sense that solutions in other industries are the real source of inspiration. With a "clean sheet" design approach and few constraints, talented individuals and teams can borrow freely from diverse industries—to devise a driverless car, a personal flying machine, or an ageless life.

Bounded innovation challenges people to overcome assumptions that are viewed as insurmountable or seen as immutable characteristics of the business. Both frugal and reverse innovation pursue solutions that start at the bottom of the pyramid,[1] but use creativity to keep getting better within their economic constraints and challenge more sophisticated markets.

The tools for inspiring focus on providing diversity of people and experiences to explore new concepts. These techniques can be combined to enhance this stage.

Companies rely on these tools to different extents. Each requires a strong culture of innovation, passionate people, and dedicated resources for people to travel, explore, and interact with relevant networks. They work best when employees can easily establish relationships across functions and across networks. Design units work best for companies that prefer to have an innovation department focused on identifying ideas. Stealth innovation is preferred for more decentralized cultures, in which resources and a passion for breakthroughs exist in every corner of the company. Bounded innovation is used when top management has a specific vision but wants to leverage the creativity of internal people—in the form of a targeted design unit, or as an open challenge to the organization. A combination of the three solutions creates the greatest value in this front-end process, although it also requires more resources. Each solution needs space to breathe, and they are rarely successful when day-to-day pressure leaves little time and resources for exploration. Table 6.1 illustrates differences among tools for inspiring.

ATTRACTING IDEAS INTO THE STARTUP CORPORATION

As you know, managing inspiration is simply the first step in supporting strategic discoveries. Companies often do not follow inspiration with putting in place the structures necessary to move strategic discoveries forward. But innovation benefits from tapping the environment not only as a source of inspiration but also as a source of ideas. What we call the "Not Invented Here" syndrome rejects ideas from the outside as irrelevant to

Table 6.1. Tools for inspiring

	DESIGN UNITS	STEALTH INNOVATION	BOUNDED INNOVATION
Boundaries	Medium	Weak	Strong
Inspiration	New interpretations of the world	New-to-the-world solutions	Bottom of the pyramid
Open networks	Study ethnographic relationships to uncover hidden needs	Identify solutions to address challenges never tackled before	Reconfigure business model using new networks

Common factors

Resources and protection from early evaluation

Supportive organizational design

Experimentation

Internal resources accessible when needed

Isolation from market and company forces

fueling the innovation process. While this syndrome was prevalent in organizations a decade ago—both in R&D departments and in market-facing departments—most companies have become aware of its limitations. Attracting ideas has become an important activity for innovation, benefiting from tools such as corporate venturing, discovery units, and innovation tournaments.

Corporate venturing scans the environment to identify startups that can potentially stoke the innovation process. Strategic acquisitions can add new products to a company's portfolio, or they can be part of an effort to craft a breakthrough solution. In the latter case, acquisitions are combined with efforts inside the company. Corporate investing provides options to promising startups that can later be integrated into the organization itself, or that can feed the larger ecosystem an organization is creating. In that instance, each investment is evaluated not on its own merit but by its contribution to the larger ecosystem.

Discovery units can be designed in different ways, but their purpose is to interact with innovators and establish relationships. Therefore they are generally located close to an innovation hub—a university, a research center, a neighborhood, or a region. Discovery units identify promising ideas and promising people and connect them with the company.

Attracting ideas from outside networks has become a fundamental process for breakthrough innovation. The tools to do so support deep engagement with innovation hubs.

Corporate venturing as a mechanism for attracting ideas requires a relatively large investment, and hence is better suited for large companies. Although medium-sized established players have used startup investing to attract ideas, their process is less structured than that of a formal corporate venture division. Corporate venturing is best suited for industries with strong entrepreneurial activity, and often requires a presence in regions where such activity takes place.

Discovery units are frequently part of an innovation department. They require dedicated people to spend time establishing relationships within relevant networks and managing partnerships. Discovery units in large companies must bridge internal and external networks. For instance, Honda's discovery unit in Silicon Valley is deeply involved in the various regional networks. But its challenge is to manage not only its relationships with those networks but also its relationship with the R&D department of Honda. The combination of fast-paced startup networks with slower-paced internal networks can be difficult.

Table 6.2. Tools for attracting

	CORPORATE VENTURING	DISCOVERY UNITS	INNOVATION TOURNAMENTS
Mechanisms to attract ideas	Investments and acquisitions	Collaboration and partnerships	Prizes
Role of managers	Identify relevant startups	Identify innovation hubs	Design and market tournaments
Role of networks	Provide access to a large number of interesting startups	Bring together a valuable set of partners	Provide ideas to the tournament

Common factors

Financial resources for prizes and investments

Strong belief in outside networks as fertile soil for ideas

Deep involvement and collaboration with outside networks

Innovation tournaments attract ideas by offering financial prizes that encourage internal and external parties to explore solutions. The framing of the question—whether it is narrow, as in addressing a specific technology challenge, or broad, as in seeking the best general breakthrough idea—determines whether the resulting ideas feed incremental or breakthrough innovation. Innovation tournaments can be single or recurring competitions, but their structure largely determines their output. Table 6.2 compares various tools for attracting ideas.

COMBINING THE PIECES OF THE STARTUP CORPORATION

The activity of combining benefits from integrating internal and external ideas—bringing elements together to craft a new business model. The more complex the strategic discovery, the more relevant this collaboration and coordination role becomes. In a reverse of the "Not Invented Here" syndrome, many established organizations seem to suffer from the "Not Able to Invent Here" syndrome. They rely on attracting ideas from outside and ignore their employees' inspirations.

Relying on external ideas—typically by collaborating with other companies or acquiring successful startups—is a powerful way to expand the portfolio of businesses into growth industries and to accelerate the innovation process. However, this strategy at times lacks an integrated solution. Without knowing how the structure of a new industry will work, and without understanding how the different pieces of the industry fit together, outsourcing the inspiration phase often leads to portfolios of interesting products that are only loosely related to each other.

Incubators are often more related to internal resources than are collaborative solutions or corporate venturing. They are a preferred solution for combining when the business model for a new innovation requires extensive experimentation. Incubators can establish relationships with external networks, but their reach is generally limited. Their structure is best adapted to moderate external coordination, limited to a few partners. Incubators efficiently work through experiments and are best suited for learning in highly uncertain environments.

Collaboration units are devoted to small partnerships and relationships with specific open networks. These units gain importance as external links become more critical. For instance, strategic discoveries that require significant contributions from universities or research centers weight these collaborative solutions more heavily. Innovation cells are related structures that integrate established companies into these critical centers of knowledge. Table 6.3 compares characteristics of different approaches to combining.

LEARNING FOR STRATEGIC DISCOVERIES

Discovering the technology and the right business model for a breakthrough requires fast experimentation cycles that max-

Table 6.3. Tools for combining

	INCUBATORS	COLLABORATION	CORPORATE VENTURING
Relevance of external networks	Medium; needed to design the business model	High; needed to access knowledge	Needed to access a large number of intersting startups
Relevance of internal links	More relevant as the incubator is embedded in the company	Relevant, although more critical in future stages	Relevant to serve the needs of business units and innovation efforts
Complexity of strategic discovery	Addresses less complex discoveries	Addresses complex discoveries with many partners	Helps bring together the pieces needed for a complex discovery

Common factors

Bring together the elements that make the breakthrough possible

Combine internal and external networks

imize learning. Prototypes are a useful way to experiment. In early stages, they do not need to be elaborate or expensive—just enough to answer the question at hand. As learning progresses, they become more detailed to address more specific questions. Prototypes are not restricted to physical products; they can also be utilized for testing assumptions of the business model: what segments of the market are potentially interested, how the product or service can be delivered, or what complementary services can be offered. Software and Internet companies use the concept of the minimum viable product to describe the most basic version of a product that can be released to the market. The minimum

Table 6.4. Tools for learning

	INCUBATORS	**DISCOVERY**	**PROTOTYPES**
Location of resources	Separate structures	Separate or within existing structures	Within existing structures
Staff	Full-time	Part-time dedication common	Part-time dedication

Common factors

Access to resources at business units, headquarters, or their networks

Heavy use of prototyping to learn

viable product often lacks many of the features that will eventually be part of the product, but it offers enough functionality to learn from customers' reactions, and it provides a platform for adding new designs and features. Its objective is to quickly enter the market to accelerate the learning from interacting with customers.

Prototyping is a central aspect of learning. Incubators, stealth innovation, and bounded innovation all rely on different types of prototyping. The learning stage requires both the resources to carry out experiments and the passion to continue despite dead ends and discoveries not fully aligned with expectations. As learning advances, prototypes often become more costly and complex. Business model experiments can require the collaboration of a number of people and organizations.

Companies that follow aggressive, play-to-win strategies use incubators in different innovation hubs around the world, as well as ones close to R&D facilities or key markets.[2] These internal structures are connected to each other, and top management supports them by tapping the resources of the larger company. Table 6.4 compares the various tools for learning.

LEVERAGING STRATEGIC DISCOVERIES

Strategic discoveries that advance to the execution stage must make the transition from an entrepreneurial to a managerial approach to organizing. An entrepreneurial approach works best while the Startup Corporation team is determining whether and how their breakthrough idea can become a business. But once the team has discovered a scalable model, scaling becomes the focus.

All three aspects of leveraging—culture, growth, and management infrastructure—are relevant to any strategic discovery. Yet their importance varies depending on the fit of the strategic discovery within the company, and the leverage of existing resources in other parts of the company. Strategic discoveries that are similar to or compatible with an existing business unit will benefit from being able to leverage the unit's existing culture and infrastructures to quickly scale. Leveraging existing resources makes fast and global deployment possible.

Strategic discoveries that do not naturally fit with existing businesses face a more difficult challenge. These Startup Corporations have to develop their cultures, growth strategies, and management infrastructures from the ground up. The team needs to decide how much of the company's culture the Startup Corporation will maintain, and how much of their culture will be unique. If the expected outcome is to become a new division of the company, the Startup Corporation will benefit from adopting the core values of the company as its own. This common ground will facilitate communication and coordination going forward. Still, even if the core values are the same, the new

---

Leveraging breakthrough innovation balances the creation of a separate business infrastructure with access to resources of current business units.

---

division's culture can have unique aspects. For instance, the new division might be more technologically driven and have a more technology-oriented local culture. Alternatively, it might have a more frugal approach to the business model, emphasizing emerging markets and cost consciousness.

Management infrastructure faces decisions similar to those surrounding culture. Strategic discoveries that will be integrated into an existing business unit benefit from using the current management infrastructure. Strategic discoveries that are likely to become a separate division or be spun off have more alternatives, either growing as an almost independent entity or leveraging existing business units' resources. The final solution generally falls in the mid-range, between independence and full leverage.

The more the Startup Corporation can leverage the existing infrastructure, the faster it can grow. However, the existing infrastructure may not fully align with the needs of the new business, and the negotiation process with business units can be difficult. At a minimum, the Startup Corporation should leverage the global presence of the established organization as well as its relationships with supply and distribution chains. From this starting point, the Startup Corporation can negotiate sharing resources as a way to deploy quickly and to lower costs in initial stages. Business units with extra resources are likely to be happy to see them used, but business units working at capacity may have a hard time finding resources to share. Such situations require a more independent approach to leveraging. Table 6.5 lists the different tools for leveraging.

INTEGRATING STRATEGIC DISCOVERIES

The three options for integrating a strategic discovery are as a new division, spinning it off as a separate company, or reconfiguring it into an existing business unit. The fit between the new business and the current corporate strategy generally determines the choice.

Table 6.5. Tools for leveraging

	CULTURE	GROWTH	MANAGEMENT INFRASTRUCTURE
Part of an existing business	Aligned with the existing business	Use the business unit's infrastructure to quickly enter markets	Fully integrated
New division or separate company	Share core values but develop local culture	Leverage certain parts of the company	Set up common interfaces
Spin-off or sale to another company	Develop own culture	Leverage but also create its own	Have independent infrastructure

Common factors

Transition from an entrepreneurial to a management attitude

Proactive management of these elements

A breakthrough product that does not alter the business–unit structure is easily incorporated into an existing business unit. Since the new product only needs to leverage resources the company already has deployed in markets, the structure of an existing business unit provides the fastest growth solution. When a breakthrough makes the product or products of a business unit obsolete, that business unit should transition to the new market. Though technically ideal, this solution can be challenging from a cultural perspective.

Spin-offs or trade sales (sales to other companies) are best suited to strategic discoveries that do not fit with a company's current strategy, or with the alternative strategies envisioned going forward. While a spin-off or trade sale captures the financial

Table 6.6. Tools for integrating

	RECONFIGURE INTO AN EXISTING BUSINESS UNIT	SPIN OFF OR MAKE A TRADE SALE	CREATE A NEW DIVISION
Characteristics of the business model	Leverages the existing business model	As trade sale, leverages existing business model in another company	Requires a new business model
Characteristics of the technology	Breakthrough technology for the business unit	Technology does not fit with current or future strategies	Technology requires a new business model
Strategic fit	Fits with the strategy of a business unit	No fit with the strategy of the company	Fits with the strategy of the company but not within an existing business unit

Common factors

Transform the management of the innovation from breakthrough to incremental

Business-unit structure becomes more adequate

Focus on capturing value

value of a strategic discovery, integrating it as a new division is the most common solution. The new division has the flexibility to design itself based on the needs of its new business model, and at the same time it does not face the challenges of transforming an existing organization. Table 6.6 contrasts the alternatives for integration.

QUESTIONS FOR ACTION

INSPIRING AND ATTRACTING

- How does my organization mix the various ways to inspire people?

- How does my organization integrate activities to inspire people with activities to attract ideas from outside?

- Does my organization create exploration teams with internal as well as external people?

COMBINING AND LEARNING

- How successfully does my organization work together with partners in innovation processes?

- What is the role of prototyping products, services, and business models in my organization?

- How can my organization better use experiments to advance innovation?

LEVERAGING AND INTEGRATING

- How much of my organization's culture should move into new business units?

- How successful is my organization in growing new business units?

- How open are managers to devoting resources to new businesses unrelated to theirs?

Innovative Cultures

7.

SINCE THE STARTUP CORPORATION lives within an established organization, the management of that organization has important implications for the success of strategic discoveries. The following chapters examine the aspects of established organizations that influence the Startup Corporation. We refer to them as the foundations, which encompass the soft aspects of culture and leadership as well as the hard aspects—strategy, incentives, and management systems. In this chapter, we focus on culture (table 7.1).

Culture can be the fertile soil that nurtures developing ideas, or it can be the hard ground that thwarts them before they have a chance to grow. Take, for example, a large Silicon Valley–based company in the software industry with a top-down, execution-focused culture. Every quarter, targets were set for each employee and closely tracked. One employee spotted an opportunity in Asia, but it required an upfront investment. At her quarterly meeting with her boss, he came with his usual list of goals for her. During their discussion, the employee told her boss about the opportunity. He did not dismiss the idea; instead, he added it to her list of goals with a 5 percent weight on her

Table 7.1. Culture as a foundation of strategic discoveries

Making resources available to innovators
Supporting people to take risks, whether they succeed or fail
Seeing breakthrough efforts as necessary to long-term survival
Balancing technology and business insights for innovation
Understanding the needs and challenges of breakthrough innovation
Openly communicating within the organization and its networks

bonus (basically making it clear that she should not spend time on it). The employee who went into her meeting with an idea to potentially help the company came out of it with more work and no additional resources to pursue it. The message was: "So, you have an idea? Great, but you can explore it only in addition to your regular job, and we'll provide you with no additional resources. Ideas worth the time and resources of the company come from top management alone." That idea was her last with the company. A culture in which people who contribute ideas end up accountable for them but have no resources to pursue them will quickly kill bottom-up innovation.

Organizations that enjoy lasting success do so in part because they have developed a strong and positive culture.[1] General Electric explained in its 2008 annual report (and featured on their website until 2012), "At GE, we consider our culture to be among our innovations. Over decades our leaders have built GE's culture into what it is today—a place for creating and bringing big ideas to life. Today, that culture is the unifying force for our many business units around the world." Google's founders thought that managing the culture of their fast-growing organizations was so important that in 2007 they added the title of chief culture officer to its human resources director, with the

Culture reflects the values and mental models that people in an organization share. Innovation and risk taking have to be part of the culture for strategic discoveries to happen.

mandate to "retain the company's unique culture and keep the Googlers happy."

Culture is "the way we do things around here." More formally, "culture comes down to a *common way of thinking*, which drives *a common way of acting*."[2] Culture is about how people *think*, which then translates into how people *behave* throughout the organization (across countries, functions, departments, and hierarchical levels as well as across time). Culture is built through years of accumulated experiences, and it is constantly evolving. Culture shapes people's reactions to issues as diverse as relying on outsiders for ideas, learning from (rather than punishing) failures, taking calculated risks, and going after hard but high-potential challenges. Innovation is fragile, and destroying an innovative culture is much easier than building one. A risk-averse, defensive company will need a powerful leader to change its culture into one conducive to fostering strategic discoveries.

CHANGING AN ORGANIZATION'S CULTURE

Altering an organization's culture requires modifying its common way of thinking, which is much easier said than done. Most "cultural change programs" fail because they ignore a counterintuitive but long-known aspect of human functioning: people act rather than think their way into new attitudes. In *Nicomachean Ethics*, written almost twenty-five hundred years ago, Aristotle explained that "we do not act rightly because we have virtue or excellence, but we rather have those because we have acted rightly. . . . Moral virtue comes about as a result of habit. . . . For the things we have to learn before we can do them, we learn by doing them, e.g. men become builders by building and lyreplayers by playing the lyre; so too we become just by doing just acts, temperate by doing temperate acts, brave by doing brave acts."[3] Reshaping the culture of an organization hence requires reshaping the behavior of enough people for long enough for them to internalize the new behavior.

Organizations can (re)shape culture through a combination of hard and soft mechanisms such as employee abilities, processes, organizational structure, performance indicators, top management behavior, information, and resource availability (table 7.2).

Applying strong and consistent alterations with any of these mechanisms can change employee behavior reasonably rapidly. However, that behavioral change trickles down into a cultural change slowly. While personal behavior can change in months,

Table 7.2. Mechanisms for shaping cultures

Employee abilities shape what individuals can do. Organizations can acquire people with specific skills, eliminate redundant ones, and train people.

Innovation activities, which focus on understanding current and future customers as well as innovative competitors (often startups), support and circulate ideas.

Goals and rewards provide the incentive to take risks and a sense of fair compensation for doing so.

Top management behavior models the important aspects of the organization and supports particular behaviors throughout the organization.

Organizational structure describes each individual's boss, peers, clients, and suppliers, clarifying individuals' organizational identity.

Access to time and resources allows people to be effective. The more resource constraints they face, the less likely employees will display expected behavior.

cultural changes may take years, depending on how big the change is, how deeply anchored the previous behaviors are, how powerful and aligned the applied forces are, how many individuals are affected, how geographically dispersed the individuals are, and how easy it is to monitor behavior and enforce changes. Management needs to be persistent and consistent over years for new behaviors to translate into a new culture.

The British-based retailer Tesco illustrates how a large organization developed a strong culture of high employee engagement, customer-focused innovation, and excellence in execution.[4] Twenty years ago, Tesco was perceived as a second-rate local organization. Since then, and despite an unsuccessful attempt to enter the US retail market, Tesco has become the third-largest and second most profitable global retailer in the world.[5]

One reason for Tesco's success has been a relentless stream of innovations. Some of these innovations have been incremental—building on the existing strategy, but executing a little better—but others have contained a significant breakthrough component. The introduction of financial services, home shopping, and branded Tesco product lines all did their part to change the market landscape.

Innovation nurtures itself by making new combinations of existing ideas. A number of Tesco's innovations were adapted from other companies' products, services, and business models, while still others came from inside. Some of the practices and mechanisms are individually quite clever, but not one alone explains the organization's remarkable growth. The difference is that Tesco has used all of them, all the time, with the same high intensity, and over several years. Tesco employees do not just "do things" to "tick the box"; they invest time and energy into each activity.

EMPLOYEE ABILITIES

To seriously pursue breakthrough innovation, recruiting talented people is crucial. While Steve Jobs is celebrated for numerous qualities (including his creative genius, extraordinary charisma, and unique sense of style), perhaps less well known is the enormous emphasis that he put on recruiting. Said Jobs, "One of the things that I've always felt is that most things in life, if you get something twice as good as average you're doing phenomenally well. Usually the best is about 30 percent better than average. . . . But what became really clear to me in my work life was that, for instance, [Steve] Wozniak was twenty-five to fifty times better than average. And I found that there were these incredibly great people at doing certain things, and you couldn't replace one of these people with fifty average people. . . . And so I have spent my work life trying to find and recruit and retain and work with this kind of people."[6] Employees' motivation to innovate is crucial, but their ability to do so is equally relevant.

Recruiting Talent

Most organizational problems start at recruitment. Zappos' founder, Tony Hsieh, is explicit about the importance of fit in the company's hiring process. In fact, he's so explicit that at the end of the company's extensive New Hire Training, trainees who are still not sure that they want to work for Zappos are given $3,000 to leave.[7] Still, this effort to find people who fit within the culture has to be balanced with the diversity that innovation demands.[8] Companies must be specific about non-negotiable qualities, but they should also ensure that these criteria allow them to recruit a set of individuals with a range of experiences, cognitive styles, and points of view. For example, L'Oréal, the world's largest cosmetics and beauty company, recruited separately for a group they called the "unconventionals"—individuals whose profiles

---

Great, diverse talent is a central piece of innovation. Careful and thorough recruiting processes, along with clear ways for people leaving the organization, are important aspects of attracting and retaining talent.

---

were interesting but who might have gathered less attention from a recruiting process often oriented toward the short-term filling of positions with specific criteria.

Both hiring and retaining individuals with high innovation potential can be challenging, as they are not necessarily the easiest people to like or to manage. These "mavericks"—who have a propensity to be innovative, independent-minded, goal-focused, and successful at risk taking—are also often more egocentric and less agreeable, behaving less as team players than average employees.[9]

Google X, Google's corporate research lab whose mandate is to "take moonshots," has recruited an impressive lineup of technical talent, including a number of top-notch academics disenchanted with academic life. These individuals combine extraordinary intellect and credentials with an equal passion for technology.[10] Having such talent on your team is never a bad thing. Still, selecting the right talent requires a careful selection process that often spans several interviews before making a hiring decision. Google and the biotech company Genentech—both consistently ranked among America's most innovative and best companies to work for—regularly put candidates through ten to twenty interviews before extending an offer.

Working with Existing Employees

An innovative culture depends on hiring talented, passionate people and then keeping them. But too often, employees' initial fervor falls victim to the forces in the organization that sap people's talent and creativity. Except in R&D units, employees typically spend most of their time and energy going after today's objectives, which are embedded in standardized processes and bound by the existing paradigm. Over time, this emphasis on optimizing existing resources reduces employees' ability to imagine other products, services, processes, or business models.

To maintain employees' passion to discover, organizations

can provide spaces for people with similar interests to meet and explore fields that initially may appear to be unrelated to the company's existing business. Exposing employees to the world outside the organization through learning expeditions on specific subjects, for example, can help staff break out of their everyday way of doing business.

By supporting external interactions, an organization enables individuals to broaden their personal and professional networks as well as be exposed to new practices and ideas. Such exploration calls for giving employees time and resources. Job rotation—which ensures that managers and other employees do not stay on any job long enough for it to become stale—is another way to maintain interest and engagement. Innovation is far more likely to happen if employee hearts and minds are involved in innovation-pursuing activities at least part of the time. While this requires employees to be willing and able to engage, it also requires managers to be willing and able to display a leadership style that supports employees' innovation efforts.

SUPPORTING INNOVATION ACTIVITIES

Once the right people are in place, nurturing activities that support innovation plays a large role in whether or not an organization innovates. Management designs the ways in which experimentation, learning, understanding customers, tracking competition and technologies, and capturing and exploring ideas all happen.

Experimentation and Learning

One of the best ways of managing risk is to experiment—through storyboarding; prototyping for inspiring, evolving, and validating ideas; and pilot testing. Netflix CEO Reed Hastings describes the company's extensive use of testing: "We are trying to set this up as a continuously learning organization. . . . My role is creating that learning atmosphere."[11] Design-thinking companies such as

Frog Design, Continuum, Luma Institute, IDEO, and SIT encourage rapid and frequent experimentation as ideas move through their design processes. Tesco is also famous for its ability to pilot ideas in a few stores, monitor the results, make adjustments, and roll out to market.

Contrast these systematic approaches to experimentation with the way the new CEO of JC Penney, Ron Johnson, attempted to turn around the declining fortunes of the retailer. Determined to take the company upmarket, in 2012 Johnson embarked on a massive change program throughout JC Penney's 1,100 stores. The change involved redesigned stores (a strategy of "stores within a store"), new marketing, and simplified pricing to replace frequent discounting, but it never gained traction. Worse, customers started to take their business elsewhere, and the company ended the year with sales down 25 percent. At an investment conference, a leading shareholder and member of the board commented, "One of the big mistakes was perhaps too much change too quickly, without adequate testing what the impact would be."[12]

Systematic emphasis on learning from experiences bolsters innovation. Process innovation, in particular, can spring from employees being encouraged to ask themselves regularly what they can learn and improve. Experimentation requires both patience and rigor, and relevant tests with appropriate resources upfront need to be set up. Without experiments, innovation is betting on a hunch—much like JC Penney did.

Focusing on Customers

Highlighting the importance of customer focus in the innovation process, Tesco's longtime CEO Terry Leahy argued that "all our innovations come from close observation of the way customers' lives are changing."[13] Similarly, Amazon's Jeff Bezos describes customer focus as a cultural issue that distinguishes Amazon from other companies, whose chiefs "craft strategy in competitive terms. When they're in the shower in the morning, they're thinking about how they're going to get ahead of one of their top competitors. Here in the shower, we're thinking about how we are going to invent something on behalf of a customer."[14] One of top management's roles is to ensure that the voice of current and future customers is heard loud and clear throughout the organization. Doing so requires employees to be regularly exposed to today's and tomorrow's customers, to the point where the customer's experience permeates the organization. Toward that end, Tesco devised the TWIST (This Week in Stores) program to give managers an opportunity to spend one week per year in stores observing and interacting with customers. The better an organization understands the experience of the customer, the better able it will be to improve that experience.

The use of "big data" also shows great potential. Tesco, for example, developed a strong lead by analyzing data generated by its loyalty cards to develop insights about its customers better and faster than their competitors. Learning about customers through the lens of big data allows Tesco to customize specific store offerings, as well as identify trends in consumer behavior.[15]

An innovative culture constantly focuses on current and future customers, innovative outside organizations, and experiments as learning tools.

While customers typically can explain what they do not like, they are often much less insightful about what they might like in the future. In fact, customers' initial tests have been negative toward breakthrough concepts that proved to be successful, such as the first Chrysler minivan and the Sony Walkman. Asking for customers' views on current and future products is not the only way—and probably not the best way—to develop products or services that truly change the existing paradigm. Henry Ford has been quoted as saying, "If I had asked customers what they wanted, they would have said 'a faster horse.'" Customers can only judge possible products based on what they already know, and sometimes what is needed is the ability to imagine what they cannot yet see.

Being Sensitive to Competition and Technology

Another aspect that shapes organizational culture is devoting time, attention, and resources to monitoring and understanding the most innovative competitors. Several times, Amazon has been a fast and efficient second to market. Amazon's MyHabit site was launched on the heels of the success of flash-sales sites such as Gilt, Groupon's momentum in daily deals led to AmazonLocal, and Amazon Mom followed Diapers.com (later purchased by Amazon). As Jeff Bezos explains, "It's very important not to be hermetically sealed. But you don't want to look at it as if, 'Okay, we're going to copy that.' You want to look at it and say, 'That's very interesting. What can we be inspired to do as a result of that?' And then put your own unique twist on it."[16]

Appreciating Employees' Ideas

Ideas are only as good as their ability to be captured, disseminated, and realized. People work on ideas if:

- they like the organization and want it to succeed
- they think the idea will be picked up
- they view the organization as open to ideas
- they have the time
- they think their contribution will be acknowledged

To foster an environment that encourages inquiry and exploration, some organizations have developed and institutionalized the "astonishment report." At the end of their induction period (generally three months), new hires are required to write and discuss with their boss a short report documenting anything and everything that they found interesting or surprising since they joined the company.

Other companies work to capture ideas from their employees by getting people together to exchange thoughts, and enabling them to connect dots across technologies and capabilities. For example, Sodexho, a world leader in the catering industry, organizes a biannual fair at which the company's 18,000-plus operating units showcase and view internal examples of innovation and best practice.[17] There are as many ways to leverage the ideas of internal employees as there are organizations (or employees!).

GOALS AND EVALUATION

In the movie *Invictus*, Nelson Mandela discusses with the captain of the South African rugby team, François Pienaar, how difficult but essential it is to inspire the team to do better than they think they can. Perhaps true of rugby, this is especially true of innovation.

One way to push employees to perform better than they think they can is to set stretch goals for the team. The Tata Nano, a car that can be sold for less than $2,500, is a case in point. Designing such a car is impossible within the existing paradigm of car design; yet the inspiring objective of making a car available to a wider range of people drove the design team to come up with unexpected solutions. Henry Ford used a similar approach to bring his Model T—far more than just a "faster horse"—to the mass market.

Stretch goals provide strong motivation for pursuing breakthrough innovation. Yet they demand time, resources, structures, and management support to be successful.

Intelligently selected stretch goals cannot be achieved by "beating the drum faster" or doing things incrementally better. They must require a breakthrough. They also require balancing tensions between different departments and collaborators to prevent the optimization of one angle at the expense of another, equally important one. To inspire and motivate, stretch goals need to be:

- important for the organization but even more crucial for society
- fun to achieve
- seen as difficult but not impossible
- simple enough for the team to visualize itself succeeding

Individuals, groups, and organizations that have previously succeeded possess the self-confidence to believe they can do it again. Less experienced groups often need help from leaders. Expressing confidence in a team's ability—and hence in the team's probability of success—can translate into actual success. Reminding groups of past achievements—including those that may not have been celebrated but were nevertheless impressive—can also boost confidence.

Team members must not spend too much time and energy fearing the consequences of not reaching their stretch targets. The more they worry about the future, the less they pursue productive endeavors. Leaders need to embrace goals but also convey that performance evaluation will be fair.

ROLE MODELS AND STRUCTURES

The culture of an organization is best reflected in the attitudes of top managers. People throughout the company look to management for cues about what behaviors are accepted. Values and company traditions that are at odds with top management behavior create unsustainable tensions. A culture that supports strategic discoveries is evident in top management's attention to fresh concepts and praise of people who take risks. In contrast, top management that says it wants innovation but penalizes risk, focuses on the short term, and shows no interest in ideas and new strategies will fail to develop innovation. The Startup Corporation is not simply a set of policies, processes, systems, and structures. It lives in a culture. Without the proper culture, these design aspects will fail.

RESOURCES, CULTURE, AND INNOVATION

The presence of excessive slack resources rarely leads to superior performance,[18] but the total absence of slack is equally problematic. In many companies, cuts to discretionary spending have gone beyond those necessary to eliminate waste. For employees to see the potential for improvement (and, even more, to allow them to pursue opportunities), they must have at least some resources to do so. Too much or too little slack inhibits innovation. Too much slack breeds complacency rather than healthy discipline, while too little slack prevents experimentation whose success is uncertain. People who fight fires ten hours a day cannot be expected to spend an extra fifteen minutes at the end of the shift contemplating how they might improve things. Setting up explicit "innovation time" when employees can explore new ideas can go a long way in fostering creativity.

Reshaping the culture of an organization requires reshaping the behavior of employees over many years, which demands consistency. Individually, the mechanisms described above will have little effect on innovation. Together, however, they can contribute to reshaping the behavior of employees in a more innovative direction and, in time, helping an organization develop a new set of innovation-supporting habits. With the nurturing of an innovative culture, the innovation paradox becomes less and less of an obstacle.

But often an organization really needs a leader.

EMPLOYEE ABILITIES

- Does my organization's recruiting process identify the best people to support the role of innovation?
- How does my organization provide support for people to enhance their innovation skills?
- How does my organization bring together people with different backgrounds to come up with innovative solutions?

ACTIVITIES AND RESOURCES

- How does my organization support experiments that advance strategic discoveries?
- What mechanisms are in place to get the most learning out of those experiments?
- What unusual practices does my organization employ to better understand customers and innovative organizations?

GOALS AND REWARDS

- Does my organization motivate breakthrough innovation by promoting and supporting stretch goals?
- What is the reward structure for people who take risks and devise valuable innovations?
- Does the culture of my organization support people who take risks and experiment, even if they fail?

ROLE MODELS AND STRUCTURES

- What is the attitude of top management toward innovation, experimentation, and learning?
- How well does the culture of my company fit with the management infrastructure regarding innovation?

8.

Leading for
Breakthrough Innovation

IF YOU ARE LEADING YOUR COMPANY toward becoming a change agent in the world, your attitude, culture, and systems all need to be attuned to that vision. A range of cultures and leadership styles support innovation, but they share the points described in table 8.1. Both soft foundations—culture and leadership—are delicate and need constant attention. Although cultures vary across companies and geographies, they all need to support risk taking and understand the role of innovation efforts. Trust in the leadership team—a fundamental aspect of every innovative organization—takes time; it develops over each decision and interaction, but it can quickly erode. Combining the operational excellence and incremental innovation needed for ongoing development with the breakthrough innovation key to future success requires leaders who possess unique characteristics.

Most managers and their organizations know how to execute. They have been doing it all their professional lives—targets are set, performance is monitored, courses of action get adjusted, and people are rewarded based on how well they perform against targets. Pursuing breakthrough innovation is different, though,

Table 8.1. Leadership as a foundation of strategic discoveries

Inspiring people to explore and experiment
Trusting people to craft new businesses
Encouraging people to trust you as a leader
Recognizing people for their efforts

and leaders must avoid letting the current strategy receive all attention and resources.

Leaders of innovative organizations provide the vision and direction but rely on their people to find the future of the company. They have faith that their people will take calculated risks to learn fast and cheap, combine internal and external talent, and learn from failure. They are confident that the future will be successful even if they don't know what that future will be, exactly. Strategic discoveries require leaders who trust that their people, rather than only themselves and top management, will find the next growth platform.

Innovative leaders also understand that participants from outside the organization are fundamental. Strategic discoveries require tapping into external networks. While some solutions to the myriad questions that putting together a new market raises will come from insiders, many others will originate with outsiders. Leaders need to provide these participants with the right incentives, engage them in each stage of the innovation process, and adapt the speed of a large company to execute with a start-up's intensity.

Strategic discoveries depend on leaders who trust their people to come up with breakthroughs. They believe that their people will innovate into the next growth platform.

Who is capable of steering a ship whose crew is adept at both exploring new territory and exploiting old? Innovation-sensitive leaders play a number of roles, and they share numerous characteristics.[1]

THE INNOVATION STRATEGIST

Helmut Panke, the ex-CEO of BMW, said, "My biggest challenge is saying 'no' to projects that are exciting, but don't fit BMW's strategy."[2] While the number of possible sources of development is almost infinite, innovative leaders must both guide the direction of exploration and, in most cases, restrict it. At the same time, they need to encourage people to innovate by giving them time to work on pet projects, pushing them to think outside the box, and listening to their ideas. For strategy, focus is important.

What does focus mean? For Lou Gerstner at IBM, focusing meant executing on a few things well. "Too many companies give up on their base business," said Gerstner. "Too many companies see their future in diversification: let's just go buy another company, that's the way to be successful. No, focus, pick something, and be very good at it."[3] For Steve Jobs, focus entailed "saying no to the hundred other good ideas that there are."[4] Focusing exploration means unambiguously identifying the things a company will *not* be doing, or the things it will stop doing. The innovation strategist must screen new ideas and make choices. Will this project make a big difference, today or tomorrow? What resources and capabilities are needed to be successful in that market? These are just a few of the questions that innovative leaders consider when choosing where to focus.

Innovation leaders also must have the courage to self-cannibalize—that is, to make their own business obsolete before others force obsolescence on them. Jeff Bezos, for example, willingly cannibalizes his companies. Amazon spent nearly $1 billion to acquire the shoe retailer Zappos in 2009, while its Amazon shoe site competed directly with Zappos. As an innovation strategist, the leader needs to recognize when it's better to compete with yourself than with someone else.

THE INNOVATION SPONSOR

Innovative leaders play many roles, only one of which is the strategist who says "no" a thousand times for every "yes." Focus doesn't have to be negative, and sponsoring innovation within an organization can be a good way to explore while staying close to areas of exploitation.

Sure, innovation occasionally occurs despite unfavorable conditions and a lack of resources. But these exceptions should not lead us to forget the majority of projects that could have been successful but failed because they were underresourced. Conversely, overresourced projects may fail because teams lose the impression of urgency.

Sponsoring innovation doesn't mean simply acting as a cheerleader. It does, however, require sustained support. Leaders should be in contact with teams regularly to maintain a sense of progress and continuity, but not so often that teams feel micromanaged. They also need to balance giving teams cover from the rest of the organization and facilitating collaboration with parts of the organization that possess resources the teams need. Organizations successfully pursuing innovation have leaders who send clear signals that failures resulting from well-designed innovation efforts will not be penalized.

Big questions for leaders often revolve around deciding

People pursuing strategic discoveries benefit from leaders who appreciate and support their efforts, recognize their contributions, and involve themselves enough to show their commitment.

whether to use an aggressive, play-to-win strategy or a more defensive, play-not-to-lose strategy:[5] how much time, energy, and resources should be allocated to exploiting—that is, orchestrating, managing, monitoring, discussing, and executing over the next twelve months—and how much should be allocated to exploring? Maintaining this balance between exploring new ground and exploiting the old is an important part of overcoming the innovation paradox. While sponsoring innovation is one way to guide exploration and spark creativity, setting the stage so that creativity occurs more regularly is another tactic.

THE INNOVATION ARCHITECT

Leaders can be personally involved in the process of innovation. Such involvement is often to ensure that employee input is being considered, or to signal that they care deeply about a particular issue. Acting somewhat like an organizational architect, the leader ensures that key processes and capabilities are developed.

While processes that keep customers in the center of employee radar screens are important, innovative leaders should also be modeling the customer focus necessary to be competitive. Michael Dell, for example, goes out of his way to visit the chat rooms and user forums to hear complaints about his company, its products, and its services. He explains, "Some of it is just chatter—you tend to filter that out. But it's so built into our system now, we actually have teams that monitor those sites routinely. It's a whole new form of feedback. It's not just noise to us."[6]

Jeff Bezos takes customer complaints a step further, using them as vehicles with which to engage employees and identify problems. Nadia Shouraboura—until recently, a vice president in charge of technology for Amazon's global supply chain and fulfillment operation—explained the rationale behind Bezos pointing out specific complaints to employees. "If one customer wrote to Jeff," said Shouraboura, "there are others who didn't. And Jeff wants to understand the screwup to make sure it gets fixed."[7]

In addition, the innovation architect finds ways to free up resources for innovation, which means knowing where to spend and where to save. For example, Amazon takes a much more frugal tack than many Silicon Valley companies. Work accommodations are plain and Bezos for a long time made low shipping rates for consumers a priority.[8] Rather than expending revenue on arguably unnecessary bells and whistles, Bezos chooses to pass on savings to Amazon customers—driving new business simply by using resources responsibly.

Regarding leadership's role in making resources available to better pursue strategic discoveries, time is the most crucial of those resources. Listed here are some of the more effective ways for an innovation architect to ensure that employees have enough time for exploration.

Support Personal Discipline and Time Management

Time and energy are finite. One executive recently explained that he got his entire management team trained to wisely use these limited resources. With his own assistant acting as "process owner" to make sure good habits get maintained, this new approach has become standard practice in his division. Time-saving approaches even include little things, such as banning Power-Point presentations in favor of six-page-maximum narratives sent in advance of meetings. Unfortunately, few organizations are active on this front, and much time and attention is needlessly wasted.

Keep Processes under Control

Equipment, technology, systems, and processes that work painlessly should be a given, but oftentimes they are not. Many organizations waste time and energy compensating for things that should work but don't. Managers too often complain about hours spent reconciling data, correcting errors, or working around systems.

'Addressing this issue requires at least two conditions. First, a widespread process orientation involving a large proportion of management and staff should internalize the idea that most activities can be organized, managed, and in many cases measured as a process. Second, management and staff must accept that effective, efficient processes demand a degree of standardization—and, therefore, some sacrifice of freedom. Processes help bring order to what otherwise can be chaos.

Eliminate Non-Value-Adding Activities

Various non-value-adding activities in organizations are inherited from the past. They were likely appropriate responses to yesterday's issues, but today many of these remnants leave people scratching their heads. The innovation architect's drive to eliminate such activities must be relentless because customer needs, staff capabilities, and available technology tend to change faster than most organizations revise their processes.

Maximize Return on Time Invested

Support functions are often criticized for generating too much bureaucracy. While most companies do not set out to create bureaucracy, they often end up doing so. The difficulty of bureaucracy is that it starts with well-intentioned people doing exactly what they were hired to do but forgetting that their job is a means to an end, not an end in itself. When the process becomes important for its own sake, it generates unnecessary work. Most organizations would benefit from being more forceful regarding activities that can—and should—be stopped.

Leaders of innovative companies must ensure that their organizations effectively free up resources for innovation and increase people's energy.

Create Effective and Efficient Decision-Making Processes

People in organizations are supposed to discuss their options, make a decision, and then execute. In reality, most discuss, decide . . . then discuss some more, decide (the same thing as the first time, or not) . . . and then they discuss again. One of our clients used to jokingly say, "We can only start really discussing something *after* a decision has been made."

Of course, reexamining decisions that were made hastily or incorrectly is beneficial. When such revisiting becomes endemic, however, an organization loses its ability to follow through on decisions, which in turn delays execution and causes frustration. Because the process itself then creates an incentive not to engage early on, but rather to wait and disrupt later, the whole cycle can become self-fulfilling.

An innovation architect ensures that decision-making processes are efficient and effective, which goes a long way toward increasing everyone's energy.

THE INNOVATION EVANGELIST

Organizations have a natural tendency to default toward exploitation and short-term focus. Leaders who strive for innovation should emphasize its importance and keep it on the agenda. Since the type and extent of innovation differ across groups of employees, the message needs to be adapted accordingly. Leaders must communicate clearly and strongly that innovation is key in going forward, presenting both sides of the need to change: the negative side ("If we don't do this, bad things will happen") and the positive ("If we do this, good things will happen").

Explain the Consequences of Failure to Innovate

Several years ago, Andy Grove, the charismatic CEO of Intel during the 1980s and 1990s, argued that "only the paranoid survive."[9] This phrase has stuck, and many other successful leaders have used it to stress the imperative of remaining hypervigilant.

More generally, leaders use four basic sources of vulnerability to emphasize the need to keep innovating.

The first, and most obvious, is competition in general. Andrew Higginson, Tesco's finance and strategy director, explained, "We stay paranoid! We have to assume that they're all out to get us, so we try to do a bit better than all of them."[10] Similarly, Tesco's then–marketing director Tim Mason noted, "Tesco is obsessed with consumers and paranoid about competitors. We have these twin things going on all the time."[11]

Some organizations have successfully used a "villain"—a competitor that receives much attention and focus—in adversarial comments, sometimes with demonizing overtones. For example, when Dell was still a glorified startup, founder Michael Dell would fire up his employees by telling them that his daughter's first words had been, "Daddy, kill IBM, kill Compaq, kill Gateway."[12] Richard Branson's relentless jabs at British Airways had a similar mobilizing effect on Virgin Atlantic employees.

Second, managers in organizations can tell stories of once successful organizations similar to theirs that subsequently failed. For example, senior managers have used the rise and fall of companies such as IBM, ABB, and Xerox to alert employees to the dangers of complacency. EMC's then-CEO Michael Ruettgers once provided a good illustration of this tactic: "We occupy a building that Prime once leased. On the second floor, there's a big auditorium. In the back of the auditorium, against a red velvet background, is a giant sign that says Prime Computer. When we moved into the building, the employees asked us to leave the sign up as a reminder of what could happen if EMC ever became complacent."[13] Highlighting global trends that could potentially threaten the business serves a similar purpose of warning about the dangers of failing to innovate.

A third source of vulnerability is the organization's history—where did the organization come from, and how did it get to this point? A few years ago, for example, the city-state of Singapore reinforced the study of local history throughout its school system. Its purpose was to remind students that, while Singapore is prosperous today, this success is an extraordinary achievement that required decades of unswerving individual discipline, collective discipline, and drive—qualities the Singapore government expects younger generations to continue to display.

The fourth avenue for innovation evangelists is to examine the organization's own vulnerabilities, highlighting sources of competitive advantage today and imagining what could wear them away. Lou Gerstner put it this way: "My view is you perpetuate success by continuing to run scared, not by looking back at what made you great, but looking forward at what is going to make you un-great, so that you are constantly focusing on the challenges that keep you humble, hungry, and nimble."[14]

Focus on the Positive

Innovation requires both passion and energy. To sustain passion, leaders need to regularly remind people of the organization's greater purpose. For example, when Apple was on the verge of collapse, Steve Jobs called a meeting to help his colleagues remember why they couldn't let Apple fail. Jobs said, "What we're about is not making boxes for people to get their job done. We believe that people with passion can change the world for the better."[15]

| Innovation needs constant reinforcement because it is not part of the day-to-day work of most organizations.

When employees succeed, they need to be recognized. Michael Dell advocates, "Celebrate for a nanosecond, then move on." Achievement at Dell is said to merit a short e-mail or a pat on the back, followed by a lengthy discussion of what could have been done better.[16] The part of this quote that tends to be emphasized is the short length of the celebration, but in many organizations success doesn't get celebrated even for a nanosecond! Leaders who strive for innovation must seize opportunities to laud progress in all its forms.

Ensure Momentum

In a study of hospitals that embarked on a continuous improvement journey, the hospitals that developed momentum by attacking easier-to-solve problems early on ended up significantly out-innovating hospitals that began by more systematically assessing various improvement possibilities.[17] Crossing a task off the to-do list can go a long way toward keeping momentum.

The ability to play these four roles is a key determinant of how successfully leaders will stimulate innovation. Remember that playing these roles well requires *time and attention*. A great deal of leaders' impact on organizations' ability to innovate comes down to how they allocate time and resources. The other major determinant is the leader's individual qualities.

PERSONAL CHARACTERISTICS OF INNOVATIVE LEADERS

No two leaders make the same strategic moves, and no two leaders think alike regarding the allocation of resources, incremental improvements, and pursuing breakthrough innovation. However, innovative leaders tend to share a handful of characteristics.

Passion

Sometimes it's not enough to make a convincing argument. You need to show feeling. Motivation for innovation comes from people passionate about what they do. Passion is infectious, and when a leader shows passion, employees see it as a quality that can get things done, and get them places. A leader must have passion for improving things, for trying new things, and for being curious in general.

At the D5 Conference in 2007, Steve Jobs talked about the importance of passion. "People say you have to have a lot of passion for what you're doing and it's totally true. And the reason is because it's so hard that if you don't, any rational person would give up. It's really hard. And you have to do it over a sustained period of time. So if you don't love it, if you're not having fun doing it, you don't really love it, you're going to give up. Oftentimes it's the ones [who] were successful loved what they did, so they could persevere when it got really tough. And the ones that didn't love it quit because they're sane, right? Who would want to put up with this stuff if you don't love it? So it's a lot of hard work and it's a lot of worrying constantly and if you don't love it, you're going to fail."[18]

Courage to Take Risks, Tolerance of Uncertainty, and Long-Term Focus

Breakthrough innovation is complex. A leader possesses both a clear vision and a focus that removes inessential complications. Vision and simplicity lower the chances of taking unnecessary risks. Since a fundamental aspect of breakthrough innovation is managing risk, a leader's attitude toward risk taking shapes the attitude throughout the company.

Another quality of innovative leaders is the ability to tolerate uncertainty and maintain a long-term focus. Like veteran pilots who know how to fly in dangerous conditions and land on most terrains, innovative leaders know how to keep their cool when the next move isn't clear.

The plan for Google X, for example, is not traditional. Astro Teller, the director of Google X, says, "If there's an enormous problem with the world, and we can convince ourselves that over some long but not unreasonable period of time we can make that problem go away, then we don't need a business plan. We should be focused on making the world a better place, and once we do that, the money will come back and find us."[19]

The differences between incremental and breakthrough innovation require leaders to apply different criteria to different projects. Yet they need to consistently communicate why varying criteria are used. Sometimes breakthroughs cannibalize existing businesses. In such cases, the organization's power structure suffers significant shifts, and trust (or lack of trust) in the leader determines whether this change will become a power struggle that threatens the company. People who are displaced but have confidence in the organization understand they will be treated fairly.

The ability to deal with uncertainty in areas over which a person has less control does not mean that leaders are relaxed. On the contrary, a great number of innovative leaders have very high standards, are incredibly driven, and possess a rare intensity of focus.

Self-Confidence

Doing something different from the status quo involves the possibility that the new product, service, or process will fail. Leaders need to be prepared to take on risk, and to sell that risk to key stakeholders. General George S. Patton said, "Self-confidence is the surest way of obtaining what you want. If you know in your own heart you are going to be something, you will be it. Do not permit your mind to think otherwise. It is fatal."[20] Leaders who strive for innovation face considerable obstacles that require strong self-confidence and belief in both their vision and their mission.

Steve Wozniak, the cofounder of Apple, explained, "First, you have to believe in yourself. Don't waver. There will be people . . . who just think in black-and-white terms. . . . Don't let these people bring you down. They only know what they're exposed to. It's a type of prejudice, actually, a type of prejudice that is absolutely against the spirit of innovation."[21] Self-confidence is one of the most crucial tools a leader can have in the face of uncertainty, risk, and competition.

Of course, the importance of self-confidence raises an important dilemma for innovative leaders. There is a fine line between being confident and arrogant, persistent and stubborn, hard-of-hearing and deaf. Leaders need to develop a "mute button" that

allows them to silence negative feedback and maintain enthusiasm and energy. They also must remain able to turn off this mute
button on occasion, to hear the feedback that can actually help
them bring a project to fruition.

I nnovative leaders share passion, an ability to accept
and manage risk, long-term focus, and self-confidence
that spread to the rest of the organization.

Innovative leaders play a number of roles in fostering an environment in which innovation thrives. Innovation strategists
need to know when to say "no" and when to say "yes," while
innovation sponsors pick projects out of the crowd to undergo
focused exploration. Innovation architects create processes that
are favorable to an innovative climate, while innovation evangelists know when to scare and when to inspire. Innovative leaders
share many qualities, though each has markedly individual lega-
cies, priorities, visions, and skills.

QUESTIONS FOR ACTION

THE LEADER AS AN AGENT OF STRATEGIC DISCOVERIES

- As a leader, how much do I trust the motivation and abilities of my people?
- How much attention do I pay to the ideas, efforts, and risk taking of my people?
- Do my people have a clear picture of the environment in which they can explore ideas?
- Do my people understand that, although most ideas will be rejected, they still need to keep innovating?
- Do I reinforce the role of innovation in the company?
- Do I regularly spend time understanding the exploration efforts of my people?
- Is my organization effective in freeing up time from non-value-adding activities for innovation?

MY PERSONAL CHARACTERISTICS AS AN INNOVATIVE LEADER

- Do I communicate my passion for the opportunities in my organization?
- Are my people passionate about these opportunities?
- Do my people trust my leadership?
- What is my attitude toward risk taking and failure?

9.

Hard Foundations
Strategy, Incentives, and Management Systems

AN INNOVATIVE ORGANIZATION requires a management infrastructure that supports the work of the leadership team as well as the culture of the company. Think about racing. If you are a team owner, and you want not simply to be competitive but to win, you need both a great driver and a great car. You may have a super driver (the leader) and a fabulous team (engineers and mechanics), but without an outstanding car you won't win. Conversely, a great car with an average driver won't get you there, either. If innovative organizations really hope to deliver, they must have soft foundations—culture and leadership—together with hard foundations—strategy, incentives, and management systems. Table 9.1 presents these hard foundations.

Strategy defines the playing field and the ambitions of the company. It defines what businesses the company is in and, more important, what businesses it is *not* in. It balances a focus on the present with investment in the future. A defensive, wait-and-see, play-not-to-lose strategy bets on the stability of the industry and the ability of the organization to react quickly to structural changes in the environment. A more aggressive, lead-the-change, play-to-win strategy looks for opportunities to create new mar-

Table 9.1. Further hard foundations of strategic discoveries

STRATEGY

> Identifying the role of incremental and breakthrough efforts

> Developing open networks to innovation hubs

> Setting boundaries that define fields to explore

INCENTIVES

> Developing fair economic incentives

> Inspiring vision that will motivate people to take risks and face uncertainty

MANAGEMENT SYSTEMS

> Establishing hiring processes that bring passionate people into the company

> Maintaining this passion through performance management systems

> Linking rich management information systems with external networks

> Governing clearly

> Creating structures to support breakthrough innovation

> Setting up budgeting processes that provide enough resources for breakthrough initiatives

kets or upset existing ones. Microsoft, for example, has followed a defensive strategy for many years, competing as a fast second in markets such as gaming devices, browsers, and mobile operating systems. The strategy has paid off in certain markets but has not been as successful as expected in others.

Retailers such as Walmart, Aldi, and Mercadona have pursued an aggressive strategy to constantly reduce distribution costs. This aggressive price reduction often upsets established brands, forcing them either to be removed from the shop floor or to significantly lower their prices. Whereas Tesla Motors, the electric car company, has followed an aggressive strategy to create a market for luxury electric cars, traditional car companies have taken a much more defensive strategy on the new technology. While some companies have presented concept cars and others have introduced them to market—like GM's Volt—their strategy is still largely to defend their fuel-engine cars; they do just enough on the electric-car front to be in the game while they wait and see how the market evolves.

Incentives also play a central role in innovation. While some analysts have put forth arguments for limiting economic incentives because they kill creativity and lead people to set narrow objectives, others believe that steep economic incentives are the reason for the success of high-growth startups.[1] Striking a balance between the two—finding what works—moves organizations in the direction of more and better innovation.

Last, management systems are the structures and processes that facilitate the exchange of information, coordination, and resource allocation. As companies grow, they must structure these functions. For instance, for employees to delve into ideas beyond the current business model, they need sufficient resources to do so, but not so many that they lose their sense of urgency. Companies such as 3M and Google allow their engineers to use work time to

---

Hard foundations—strategy, incentives, and management systems—are a necessary complement to the soft foundations of innovative leaders and cultures. Organizations that have one without the other will often fail at innovation.

---

explore. This type of policy is an institutional design decision that supports creativity.

Each of these hard foundations—strategy, incentives, and management systems—plays an important role in the ability of an organization to foster breakthrough innovations as well as develop market-grabbing incremental innovations.

STRATEGY FOR BREAKTHROUGH INNOVATION

Strategic plans within traditional business units are often incremental, designed to further advance the reach of existing business models. They start with an analysis of the current industry that assumes that the forces shaping the markets will be comparable going forward. These plans further assume that the past strengths of the organization will carry on into the future. The intersection of industry projections and company strengths leads to a strategy that is largely an evolution of the already existing one. Such a strategy tells the company how to move forward on its current path.

The typical strategic planning process of an engineering company illustrates this point. It starts with the head of the company providing divisions with growth and profit expectations for the coming year. These expectations are somewhat above industry growth estimates—the goal being to gain market share. Next, each divisional manager analyzes the markets of her division, including both customers and competition. Then she analyzes the strengths and weaknesses of the division. Finally, each divisional manager discusses her plan to meet the set financial goals. Even if the company has significantly grown internationally, entering new markets is not always contemplated as part of the strategic plan.

This sort of process does not even begin to encompass breakthrough innovations. Breakthrough innovations cannot be planned because they involve too much uncertainty. Yet planning is essential for companies to continue delivering value.

Companies that play defensively craft their strategies to further advance their current business model. The resource allocation process devotes most resources to building additional competitive advantage against existing competitors—the unspoken bet being that the industry will remain stable, and the best use of resources is to strengthen position, gain market share, and capture a higher percentage of industry value. Such companies' attitude toward the possibility of structural changes that may upset existing market structures is to, more or less, wait and see. Their main objective regarding market shifts is to have enough knowledge and resources *not to lose* when large changes take place. By investing small quantities in technologies, startups, and networks that could lead the change, their aim is to adapt quickly to the new industry structure if and when it comes. Companies often expect these investments to be enough to give them a head start on the road to becoming fast seconds.

Companies that play aggressively plan their strategy to keep competing successfully, but they devote more attention and resources to creating new markets and upsetting existing ones. They design two strategies simultaneously, one for the current value proposition and another to explore growth opportunities. The two are ultimately related in their quest for growth, but they are very different. While the first is traditional—paying particular attention to industry analysis matched against the capabilities of the organization—the second focuses on breakthrough innovation, often combining strategic bets with strategic discoveries.

Making strategic bets involves constantly scouting the environment for new opportunities and trends. Top management attains to radical ideas by acquiring promising startups and forging alliances with technology centers. These initial efforts are often well supported with additional investment and access to complementary assets, helping to quickly scale these businesses.

For example, Sam Palmisano, IBM's CEO from 2002 until 2012, regularly asked scientists at the company to identify potentially influential technology trends that could shape the world in ten years. Once a year, he held a day-long discussion with the directors of IBM labs to consider the longer-term future and prepare the company to build markets based on those future technologies. In 2002, these discussions predicted the importance that data management (big data), cloud computing, social businesses, and mobile technology would have going forward; they ultimately led IBM to further deemphasize hardware, and to acquire a set of companies in the data management and data analysis spaces.[2] In 2008, IBM's top management took an additional step ahead and made the strategic bet to focus the scientific resources of the company—$6 billion a year invested on R&D, laboratories around the world, more patents per year than any other company, and five Nobel Prize winners—on addressing long-term big business and social challenges, including energy, pollution, health care, and transportation.[3]

Frugal innovation offers another perspective on markets and technology. It focuses on segments that have been traditionally ignored as too impoverished to be profitable. Frugal innovation stresses affordability and sustainability, the objective being to reduce or eliminate unnecessary costs to serve these emerging markets.[4] For instance, the Indian industrial group Godrej & Boyce has developed a battery-run refrigerator, the ChotuKool ("little cool" in English), that retails for $70.[5] It is large enough to hold just a few items, because people in village huts do not buy in bulk and tend to shop every day. ChotuKool uses desktop computer technology to cool rather than the traditional compressor, and the battery protects the refrigerator from frequent power outages.[6] Even when the immediate objective is to meet the needs of emerging markets, the learning that comes from designing for nontraditional segments has powerful implications for traditional segments as well.

The Tata group has also used strategic bets to lead emerging market innovations with a large breakthrough component, including the Tata Nano car and a water purification device that retails for less than $30. In cases like these, top management often proposes a challenging goal that can be achieved only if traditional assumptions are broken and breakthrough ideas are implemented. Top management then puts together a team with the right resources to pursue the goal.

Aggressive strategies incorporate strategic discoveries by making resources available to creative people in the organization; these people are then better able to explore radical ideas and the various ways an organization can exploit them. The play-to-win strategy involves putting limits on these explorers; leaders set the boundaries of the playing field, which helps an organization avoid dispersing its efforts. The Swiss pharmaceutical company Novartis has defined its boundaries for exploration around small, carefully defined groups of patients. It believes that smaller but more numerous searches will lead to more effective therapies with fewer side effects.[7] While top managers may not always be able to predict where new discoveries will happen, they can certainly focus on a given territory.

Resource allocation for strategic bets and strategic discoveries should be separate from investments made toward maintaining the organization's position in the market. Because of its inherent risk, breakthrough innovation will frequently lose to incremental projects when they are compared using financial metrics. Having discrete budgets for different innovation efforts keeps incremental innovation from crowding out breakthrough innovation. For example, the German technology company Siemens has a policy of setting aside about 5 percent of its total R&D budget to investigate long-term technologies, develop road maps, and predict long-range technology scenarios. Projects within this 5 percent do not compete for funding against incremental projects, and this separate budgeting has generated insights that have pushed the company into new businesses, including personalized health care.[8]

The innovation budget varies with the innovation strategy of each company. A play-not-to-lose strategy will heavily weight resource allocation toward incremental innovation, often using more than 90 percent of the budget and leaving a mere 10 per-

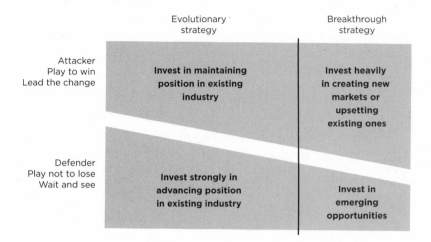

	Evolutionary strategy	Breakthrough strategy

Figure 9.1. Budget proportions of play-to-win
and play-not-to-lose strategies

cent for pursuing breakthroughs. A company following a play-to-win strategy, on the other hand, will usually put closer to 70 percent of its overall budget toward incremental innovation and operational efficiency, staking the rest in longer-term goals (figure 9.1).

Larry Page, the founder of Google, has suggested a 70–20–10 ratio: 70 percent of the budget devoted to existing strategies and incremental innovation, 20 percent directed toward mid-range goals, and 10 percent given to the exploration of future breakthrough innovation. This budget includes internal as well as open network investments. While this budget proportioning works for an established player such as Google, different markets and conditions call for other budget strategies.

Aggressive strategies provide more support for people to pursue strategic discoveries, as the company believes in its ability to create new markets.

179

While overall organizational strategy is an important hard foundation, motivating employees to perform is another important crucial aspect of overcoming the innovation paradox.

INCENTIVES FOR BREAKTHROUGH INNOVATION

Amazon's cash compensation for executives is relatively low compared to that of other companies. It relies on stock ownership both to reward performance and to convey the message that success depends on teamwork. While the stock performance has certainly helped retention, it is not perceived as the most important factor for Amazon's recruiting efforts. "You go to Amazon because there's something big going on," said a recently departed executive working on a startup of his own. "Other companies pay more."

Extrinsic motivation has to do with pursuing a certain objective because of the payoff associated with achieving it. It's what kicks in when we give commissions to salespeople or provide economic incentives to managers. Salespeople may enjoy selling, in much the same way that managers like corporate life, but the additional compensation they receive if they meet objectives motivates them to go the extra mile.

But innovation is different. People generally do not chase breakthrough innovation and run the risk of failing it entails because they might get extra compensation if they succeed. Motivation for pursuing innovation involves passion. People go after breakthrough innovation and work long hours because they believe in their idea and are fervent about it. Whether it be passion for a product, a new business model, a new industry, or a better society, it usually involves believing that whatever is being pursued will change the way we live in some way.

Intrinsic motivation is this internal drive to pursue objectives for the pure satisfaction of achieving them. Amazon founder Jeff Bezos has said, "You don't choose your passions; your passions choose you."[9] When people are impelled by passion, they may still fail, but that failure is taken as a temporary setback, not a definitive end. Winston Churchill described success as "moving from failure to failure without losing enthusiasm," and the advice for technology startups is to go after passion and the money will follow.[10]

Vision and Values

Vision and values—known collectively as belief systems[11]—inspire people to use their energy and creativity to pursue a worthwhile goal. Design departments of fashion firms, for example, are especially careful in shaping their work environment. To guide designers' efforts, they set a theme for a particular collection and then provide inspiration for that theme: trips to places associated with it, picture collages, books and archives, and networking events to align the theme with the market. The chief designer's leadership also reinforces inspiration.

A company's vision, if used well, motivates people not only to excel in their daily jobs but also to constantly seek fresh ideas. Akiro Morita, Sony's cofounder, started the company to establish a great place for engineers to work, to make "Made in Japan" a sign of quality, to be the first Japanese company to distribute directly in the US, and to create products that are found world-wide. He said, "Our plan is to lead the public with new products rather than ask them what kind of products they want. The public does not know what is possible, but we do."[12]

Maximizing shareholder value is hardly a vision that inspires people to create and take risks. Saving lives, improving quality of life, changing the way people shop, or putting information at people's fingertips, however, are all perceived as worthy of effort. In the same way that fashion designers need a theme to guide their creativity, companies need a vision and a purpose if they truly want to innovate.

Economic Incentives

The role of passion and vision in innovation is evident in startup companies. Founders and early employees are intensely passionate and put in long hours pursuing their vision (and almost all founders believe that their ideas will succeed).

Of course, not only passion and vision drive founders. Those who start a for-profit company also believe that their concept will make them money. Economic incentives are important, and the incentive structure of startups often gives a large piece of company equity to the founders. If a startup succeeds because the idea was great and it was well executed, the founders are handsomely rewarded. In these cases, economic incentives play a crucial role. If founders received a fixed salary instead of a significant portion of the equity, their fervor might quickly fade.

Startup founders are driven by passion, but they know they will be fairly rewarded if their scheme generates value. No founder of a failed startup complains about not having made money; they know it is part of the game. The equity position provides them with a fair economic reward whether the company succeeds or fails. Venture capitalists are careful not to drop the startup management team's equity portion too low. If founders feel they are not fairly rewarded, they may lose their passion.

For passion to drive innovation, economic incentives must be perceived as fair. This perception can translate into a sizeable variable part to reward success.

When extrinsic motivation is conspicuous, intrinsic motivation can become irrelevant. In other words, money can become a greater motivator than the original purpose. Extrinsic motivation can become salient because it is either too low or too high—an important note, since intrinsic motivation is crucial for innovation. One alternative is to eliminate economic incentives. In certain settings, a flat salary may be the best way to compensate creative people. But in most circumstances, it will not.

Strategic discoveries demand many hours beyond the regular working day. Even outside work, an innovator's brain is almost constantly tweaking an idea. Breakthrough innovation requires the social skills to create internal support and external networks to experiment with the model. It also requires taking risks—the risk of failing, but also such risks as leaving a comfortable career path to try something uncertain. If all this energy is rewarded with a mere fixed salary and the value generated by the breakthrough is not shared, the particular person or team responsible for the breakthrough learns that the company is good at sharing efforts but not at sharing the value created by them. Compensation is not simply a transfer of money; it is a symbol of recognizing effort.

The end rewards for people engaged in projects that can eventually create breakthroughs must be perceived as fair—which often means variable compensation associated with overall success (rather than at interim milestones). Creative people know that being part of exploratory projects will require long hours at the fringes of the company while the rest of the organization focuses on execution. Economic rewards are necessary, but social rewards such as promotions or access to resources to pursue new ideas also serve as good incentives. Signs of recognition and appreciation are highly valued as well. For instance, one Silicon Valley company provides tickets to a game of the local National Hockey League team whenever an important milestone is achieved. These signs show that management is aware of people's extra effort and risk taking to move the company forward (figure 9.2).

While breakthrough innovation comes from passionate people, the organization has to provide a compelling vision and fair rewards for that passion to thrive. The perception of what is a fair reward will of course vary across companies, professions, geographies, and cultures. As strategy and incentives surrounding breakthrough innovation differ from organization to organization and industry to industry, so do management systems.

Figure 9.2. Rewards for supporting passion

MANAGEMENT SYSTEMS FOR BREAKTHROUGH INNOVATION

Beyond strategy and incentives, management systems and processes create the structure that supports breakthrough innovation. The influence of these systems starts with the people who are hired. Hiring policies determine whether the workforce represents a good mix of talent and diversity: those who execute and those who explore, the focused and the plugged-in. Research has proven that innovation is more likely to happen when people from different disciplines who have varying expertise and views come together. The culture of the organization will in large part determine whether diversity reinforces collaboration or creates camps that do not talk to each other. Management systems work together with culture to stimulate exploration efforts and transform them into valuable innovations. Policies that support exploration efforts include communicating strategic boundaries, allocating resources for exploration, and holding events and gatherings that connect dissimilar people, strengthening ties to external networks.

Siebel Systems, for example, had clear boundaries that focused on software, customer relationship management, and customer satisfaction. This clarity regarding its purpose and its markets helped them dominate—until, of course, this strategy proved to be unfit for the changes in the industry's structure.

Intuit, the accounting and tax software company, has formalized its connections to external networks by constantly interacting with customers and inviting promising startup companies to its headquarters—to learn both about them and about possible partnerships.[13] Scott Cook, the founder of Intuit, decided that leveraging customers to build content was an important part of innovation. Yet he knew as well that ideas on how to involve external people needed to come from employees throughout the company. He provided the challenge, set the boundaries, and then let people experiment—exploring other successful companies, trying novel ways of doing things. He also protected the experiments from being routinized by the everyday operations of the organization.[14]

Such systems and processes structure the early stages of a new concept. The way they are designed ultimately influences whether these ideas become visible too soon—which may kill or mutate them into incremental innovations by strategies focused on execution—or have enough "under-the-radar" breathing space before they are exposed to the rest of the company. At Apple, Steve Jobs prolonged the secrecy of breakthrough projects almost until their release to market. This attitude was directed not only toward the external world but also inside the company in the form of off-limits areas and the threat of being fired if product launch copy made it into the wrong hands.[15]

Management systems further control the flow of ideas through the selection process. For instance, idea fairs are ways to select concepts based on the wisdom of the company's crowd: those that get the most votes receive additional resources. Gillette, for example, used innovation fairs at which units displayed their most promising concepts—everything from new shaving products for women to new methods for the legal department to highlight ethical standards.[16]

M anagement systems provide the
infrastructure for information and resources
to flow to decisionmakers and innovators.

Alternatively, processes can be set up to move ideas to top management, who then decide which ones get additional funding. Infosys, the Indian software giant, invites young high performers to eight of their management meetings in what they call "the 30/30 rule": "30 percent of the participants in a strategy discussion should be younger than age 30, because they are creative and not wedded to the past." The company also invites clients to one-on-one meetings in which clients can challenge assumptions and offer ideas for growing the company. Additionally, Infosys hosts get-togethers with unique structures like strategy graffiti walls and jam sessions around strategic questions such as how to win in emerging markets. These structured processes to gather ideas at Infosys have led to important incremental innovations, such as banking software, but also to promising breakthrough ideas that became R&D projects in fields such as health care and education.[17]

The ramp-up of a new business model that can develop operational excellence as well as foster breakthroughs needs to leverage the muscle of the company. Integrating these efforts within the larger framework of the organization requires systems and processes. The management of breakthrough activities—from exploring new ideas to fitting them into the larger organization— demands an overall view of the pipeline of projects. Measurement and information systems provide the relevant information for that view.[18]

QUESTIONS FOR ACTION

STRATEGY

- Does my organization use a play-to-win or a play-not-to-lose strategy?

- Does my organization have separate planning for improving existing strategies and exploring new ones?

- Does my organization have a separate budget to support breakthrough innovation?

- How would I change the planning process to better support breakthrough innovation?

- How would I describe the vision and values of the company? Are they inspiring?

INCENTIVES

- How does my organization reward people who take the effort and risk to explore new opportunities?

- How do people in my organization perceive the incentives for breakthrough innovation?

- How passionate are people in my organization?

- What does my organization do to maintain and increase this passion?

MANAGEMENT SYSTEMS

- How do my company's recruiting policies support diversity?

- What systems does my company use to induce people with different backgrounds to interact and explore?

- What systems are in place at my company to flow ideas to the right people and resources to the ideas?

- What systems does my company employ to manage the discovery and leverage stages of innovation?

10. Wrapping Up

MANY ESTABLISHED COMPANIES have a unique combination of access to networks, global presence, knowledge, resources, and management expertise that makes them well positioned to address the complex challenges that our societies face. Making progress toward solutions to these issues will require breakthrough thinking. Simply extrapolating our current business and social models will be far from enough. Yet the coming of age at roughly the same time of two trends—the emergence of a huge technological shift and the rise of venture capital funding— has created the myth that established companies cannot bring breakthrough innovations to market. Although this myth holds true for many companies, others have proven it wrong.

The innovation paradox reflects how a narrow understanding of innovation has led many established players to believe in this myth—which has become a self-fulfilling prophecy. Over the decades the relentless focus on efficiency, execution, and short-term financial goals has reinforced the business unit as the preferred organizational structure. The business unit has proven to be the most effective management approach to deliver on these dimensions. As we have said before, it is hard to argue against efficiency, quality, and flexibility.

Of course, business units are innovative; they need to be to remain competitive. But the innovation they support is largely incremental, advancing existing technologies and business models in an effort to gain a lead over competitors. As companies rightly push the business–unit management model and believe that they are creative because they bring incremental ideas forward, they are at the same time often blocking themselves from the possibility of breakthrough innovation.

Breakthrough innovation works with a different management model than does the traditional business unit. Rather than valuing efficiency and short-term financial goals, it encourages discovery and vision. It does not call for planning in the traditional sense, but it emphasizes searching across diverse environments, and it encourages experimentation in both technology and business models. These objectives are at odds with those that make business units and incremental innovation successful, and the frustration of established companies to come up with breakthroughs is the result of this tension. Business units innovate, and business units want breakthroughs, but their processes are designed to deliver incremental innovation.

Some innovative companies are led by charismatic and visionary CEOs. While visionary CEOs have dramatically different views of the future than most, they still need organizations that execute them well. These organizations share many characteristics of the business unit. However, despite such leaders, bottom-up breakthrough innovation is often blocked.

The drawback of top-down breakthrough innovation—what we've called strategic bets—is that visionary business leaders seldom succeed several times. If the first vision is right, but the second vision is wrong, the management model can drive the company against a brick wall, leaving little room for dissension within the company. Of course, there are exceptions, and some

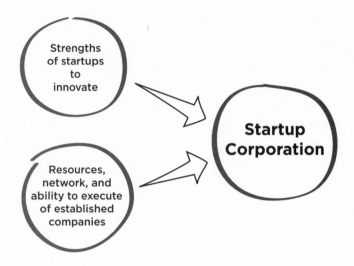

Figure 10.1. The Startup Corporation

entrepreneurs have scored wins more than once. But frequently the success of the first breakthrough is unrelated to the quality of the second.

Strategic discoveries, however, are bottom-up breakthrough innovations. They involve tapping the brainpower within the company and its networks to allow breakthroughs to bubble up. Strategic discoveries require a different management approach from that of the business unit—an approach embodied in the Startup Corporation. While this management structure is inspired by the stages of innovation that startups follow, it leverages the strengths associated with being part of an established company (figure 10.1).

Strategic discoveries will rarely beat startups at what they do best: creating breakthroughs in specific products and services. Established companies generally do not have startups' speed, and they are not exposed to market forces in the way startups are. Strategic discoveries will not beat science in coming up with breakthrough technologies, either. However, strategic discoveries excel at fostering breakthrough innovations that involve complex combinations of technologies, markets, and networks—innovations at the system level rather than the product or service level. Obviously, such discoveries also need product- and service-level innovations, but as part of a more complicated attempt at redefining industries or creating new ones.

Strategic discoveries simply do not happen within business units. Strategic discoveries need to be managed, and the Startup Corporation is the management model for nurturing them. Because the Startup Corporation is situated within an established company, the soft and hard foundations of the company are paramount. A perfectly designed Startup Corporation model will still fail if its surrounding culture provides no incentives for risk taking (figure 10.2).

The successful implementation of the Startup Corporation model combines insights from startups with the advantages of being part of an established company. Startups are founded on the following principles: be exposed to different environments; copy and combine to learn and invent; migrate ideas to new contexts; link people and ideas; communicate and share; take risks; play with new combinations; and leverage your networks. Because moving from a seed idea into a fully scalable business requires discovering the many aspects that will finally shape the business,

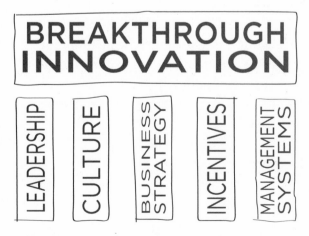

Figure 10.2. Designing for breakthrough innovation

activities leading to successful startups are not sequential. Rather, startups go back and forth as they experiment and craft their business model. Market forces dominate most of these activities, and the local market determines the level of stimulation for ideas.

In designing the Startup Corporation, established companies need to consider how they will manage the process of innovation. How will they inspire their people and people in their networks to come up with breakthrough ideas? Because of the importance of ecosystems for strategic discoveries, the Startup Corporation model utilizes tools—from collaboration with research institutions to startup acquisition—to attract contributors to the breakthrough. Both the stages of innovation and the design of the Startup Corporations substantially replicate market forces.

Ultimately the strength of established companies is their excellence at managing complexity. Combining different ideas, resources, and external and internal players builds on this management ability. Different solutions mix resources in various ways. Experiments test these solutions to learn which model will be best suited for getting the innovation to market. Figure 10.3 illustrates the activities that need to be managed to get breakthrough innovation.

Initial releases to market often need refinement, but incremental innovation is the strength of business units. At this point, the Startup Corporation leverages the rest of the company to move quickly through the cycles of incremental innovation and grow the market. When the innovation is mature enough that keeping ahead of competitors requires the business units' skills—execution and incremental innovation—the final stage has come.

INSPIRE ATTRACT COMBINE LEARN LEVERAGE INTEGRATE

Figure 10.3. Managing strategic discoveries with the Startup Corporation

Various organizational designs and tools address each of these activities. Every alternative relies on market and organizational forces in different ways, and a well-designed Startup Corporation will incorporate these options according to its own situation: its size, its internal strengths and weaknesses, and its industry. In developing breakthroughs, often the main weakness is to fail at managing the entire innovation process. Companies devote many resources and much attention to the early stages—the more visible, inspirational, and spectacular ones—but they frequently fail to follow up. They fall into the Xerox PARC trap, in which they originate great ideas that end up with somebody else. Other organizations avoid the expenses necessary to foster real breakthroughs and find themselves incrementally innovating for vanishing markets, while still others have ideas that they simply can't bring to market. This is the innovation paradox at work, and the Startup Corporation is best suited to respond to its challenge.

Governments can shape an environment that nurtures or inhibits innovation, but they do not make innovation happen. Research centers will remain at the forefront of technology and science, but their breakthroughs still need to be brought to the market. Startups will continue to surprise us with amazing breakthrough products and services, but managing the complexity of combining multiple sources of innovation, channeling the geniuses in organizations and society toward a better world, and doing it all to scale within established companies is the job of the Startup Corporation.

NOTES

PREFACE

1. J. Lerner, *The Architecture of Innovation: The Economics of Creative Organizations* (Boston: Harvard Business Review Press, 2012).

2. L. Bossidy and R. Charan, *Execution: The Discipline of Getting Things Done* (New York: Crown Business, 2002).

3. G. P. Pisano and D. J. Teece, "How to Capture Value from Innovation: Shaping Intellectual Property and Industry Architecture," *California Management Review* 50 (1): 278–296; R. Adner, *The Wide Lens: A New Strategy for Innovation* (New York: Penguin Group, 2012).

4. M. Gladwell, "The Televisionary," *The New Yorker*, May 27, 2002.

5. For additional arguments on the challenges to breakthrough innovation among established companies, see G. C. O'Connor, A. Corbett, and R. Pierantozzi, "Create Three Distinct Career Paths for Innovators," *Harvard Business Review* 12 (2009): 78–79.

6. T. Kelley and J. Littman, *The Ten Faces of Innovation: IDEO's Strategies for Defeating the Devil's Advocate and Driving Creativity Throughout Your Organization* (New York: Currency Doubleday, 2005).

CHAPTER 1: WHAT IS THE INNOVATION PARADOX?

1. R. Jana, "Inspiration from Emerging Economies," *Businessweek*, March 23, 2009.

2. J. Nocera, "How Not to Stay on Top," *The New York Times*, August 19, 2013.

3. For more on the concept of disruptive innovation and disruptive technology, see C. M. Christensen, *The Innovator's Dilemma: When New Technologies Cause Great Firms to Fail* (Boston: Harvard Business School Press, 1997).

4. J. Goldenberg, R. Horowitz, A. Levav, and D. Mazursky, "Finding Your Innovation Sweetspot," *Harvard Business Review* 3 (March 2010): 120–129.

5. For companies' potential reaction to these disruptions, see C. C. Markides

and D. Oyon, "What to Do Against Disruptive Business Models (When and How to Play Two Games at Once)," *MIT Sloan Management Review* 4 (Summer 2010): 25–32.

6. This approach to thinking about innovation was originally formulated by Robert Shelton. See T. Davila, M. J. Epstein, and R. Shelton, *Making Innovation Work: How to Manage It, Measure It, and Profit from It* (Upper Saddle River, NJ: Prentice Hall, 2013).

7. Different companies and authors label this matrix using different terms. The *y* axis has been referred to as assets or technology and the *x* axis as markets or competitive impact. The distinction between incremental and breakthrough innovation and the differences in between have been referred to as core (similar to incremental), adjacent (incremental with a breakthrough component to it), and transformational (similar to breakthrough). Incremental has also been labeled sustaining innovation, and breakthrough has been labeled as radical, game changer, or emerging business areas. See B. Nagji and G. Tuff, "Managing Your Innovation Portfolio," *Harvard Business Review* 5 (May 2012): 68–74; M. W. Johnson and A. G. Lafley, *Seizing the White Space: Business Model Innovation for Growth and Renewal* (Boston: Harvard Business Press, 2010). For an in-depth analysis of business model innovation through adding novel activities, linking activities in novel ways, or changing who performs different activities, see R. Amit and C. Zott, "Creating Value through Business Model Innovation," *MIT Sloan Management Review* 3 (2012): 41–49.

8. D. K. Rigby, K. Gruver, and J. Allen, "Innovation in Turbulent Times," *Harvard Business Review* 6 (June 2009): 79–86. These authors further develop the idea of combining creativity and business at the leadership level.

9. Ibid.

10. C. Markides and P. A. Geroski, *Fast Second: How Smart Companies Bypass Radical Innovation to Enter and Dominate New Markets* (San Francisco: Jossey-Bass, 2004).

11. M. Tripsas, "Everybody in the Pool of Green Innovation," *The New York Times*, November 1, 2009.

12. J. Menn, R. Waters, and D. Gelles, "Jobs Biography Reveals Apple Recipe for Success," *Financial Times*, October 25, 2013.

13. R. Stross, "The Auteur vs. the Committee," *The New York Times*, July 23, 2011.

14. J. H. Dyer, H. B. Gregersen, and C. M. Christensen, "The Innovator's DNA: Five 'Discovery Skills' Separate True Innovators from the Rest of Us," *Harvard Business Review* 12 (2009): 61–67.

15. Davila, Epstein, and Shelton, *Making Innovation Work*.

16. W. Kuemmerle, "Foreign Direct Investment in Industrial Research in

the Pharmaceutical and Electronics Industries—Results from a Survey of Multinational Firms," *Research Policy* 28, nos. 2–3 (1999): 179–193; C. A. O'Reilly, J. B. Harreld, and M. L. Tushman, "Organizational Ambidexterity: IBM and Emerging Business Opportunities," *California Management Review* 51 (2009): 4.

17. We do not discuss how to push top-down incremental innovation. That issue is addressed in such excellent management books as R. Simons, *Performance Measurement and Control Systems for Implementing Strategy* (Upper Saddle River, NJ: Prentice Hall, 1999).

18. On the idea of risky moves from top management, see R. Charan and M. Sisk, "Strategic Bets," *Strategy + Business* 63 (2011).

CHAPTER 2: THE BENEFITS AND LIMITS OF THE BUSINESS UNIT

1. A. D. Chandler Jr., *Strategy and Structure: Chapters in the History of the American Industrial Enterprise* (Cambridge, MA: MIT Press, 1962).

2. J. Birkinshaw and M. Mol, "Management Innovation: A Problemistic Search Perspective on Why Firms Introduce New Management Practices," *Journal of Business Research* 62 (12): 1269–1280.

3. J. M. Utterback, *Mastering the Dynamics of Innovation* (Boston: Harvard Business School Press, 1994).

4. Walmart has changed its slogan to "Save money. Live better."

5. F. E. Allen, "The Terrible Management Technique That Cost Microsoft Its Creativity," *Forbes*, July 3, 2012.

6. R. Simons, *Performance Measurement and Control Systems for Implementing Strategy* (Upper Saddle River, NJ: Prentice Hall, 1999).

7. J. Schumpeter, "Think Different," *The Economist*, August 6, 2011.

8. A. G. Lafley, "What Only the CEO Can Do," *Harvard Business Review* 5 (May 2009): 54–62.

9. B. Stone and S. Ray, "Don't Dream It's Over," *Bloomberg Businessweek*, January 28, 2013.

10. See T. Davila, M. J. Epstein, and R. Shelton, *Making Innovation Work: How to Manage It, Measure It, and Profit from It* (Upper Saddle River, NJ: Prentice Hall, 2013).

CHAPTER 3: THE SUCCESS OF STARTUPS

1. M. Zwilling, "8 Innovation Secrets from Steve Jobs," *Business Insider*, September 29, 2010.

2. C. Winter, "How Three Germans Are Cloning the Web," *Bloomberg Business Week*, February 29, 2012.

3. U. Lichtenthaler, M. Hoegl, and M. Muethel, "Is Your Company Ready for Open Innovation?" *MIT Sloan Management Review* 1 (Fall 2011): 45–48.

4. J. Reingold and D. Burke, "Can P&G's CEO Hang On?" *Fortune*, February 25, 2013, 66–75.

5. L. Kramer, "How French Innovators Are Putting the 'Social' Back in Social Networking," *Harvard Business Review* 10 (October 2010): 121–124.

6. T. Brown, "Change by Design," *Businessweek*, October 5, 2009.

7. E. Ries, *The Lean Startup: How Today's Entrepreneurs Use Continuous Innovation to Create Radically Successful Businesses* (New York: Crown Business, 2011). Also see S. Blank and B. Dorf, *The Four Steps to the Epiphany* (Pescadero, CA: K&S Ranch Press, 2012).

8. John Erceg, founder of Budgetplaces.com, personal communication.

9. A. Rajaraman and A. Davila, "Scripped.com: Creating the Business Model," IESE Case E-146-E, 2012.

10. L. Pujol, S. Alvarez de Mon, and A. Davila, "Weizmann Institute: Creating the Future of Science," IESE Case E-156-E, 2012.

CHAPTER 4: THE STARTUP CORPORATION

1. S. Lohr, "Who Says Innovation Belongs to the Small?," *The New York Times*, May 24, 2009.

2. N. Radjou and J. Prabhu, "Mobilizing for Growth in Emerging Markets," *MIT Sloan Management Review* 52, no. 3 (Spring 2012): 81–88. This reference includes other examples of large corporations, such as GE and Xerox, that are using their muscle to devise breakthrough innovations.

3. For example, see C. F. Munce, "Venture Capital: Getting Past the 'Winning Company' Approach," *Business Week Online*, July 23, 2009, 5.

4. H. W. Chesborough, *Open Innovation: The New Imperative for Creating and Profiting from Technology* (Boston: Harvard Business School Press, 2005).

5. A. G. Lafley and R. Charan, *The Game-Changer: How You Can Drive Revenue and Profit Growth with Innovation* (New York: Crown Business, 2008).

6. For a detailed article on the innovation process, see S. L. Beckman and M. Barry, "Innovation as a Learning Process: Embedding Design Thinking," *California Management Review* 50, no. 1 (Fall 2007): 25–56.

7. J. H. Dyer, H. B. Gregersen, and C. M. Christensen, "The Innovator's DNA: Five 'Discovery Skills' Separate True Innovators from the Rest of Us," *Harvard Business Review* 12 (2009): 61–67.

8. R. I. Sutton, *Weird Ideas That Work: How to Build a Creative Company* (New York: Free Press, 2002).

9. "How Seemingly Irrelevant Ideas Lead to Breakthrough Innovation," Knowledge@Wharton.upenn.edu, January 30, 2013.

10. A. Shapiro, "Stop Blabbing About Innovation and Start Actually Doing It," www.FastCompany.com, accessed April 16, 2012.

11. W. J. Holstein, "Hotbeds of Innovation," *Strategy and Business*, January 24, 2011.

12. E. J. Malecki, "Connecting Local Entrepreneurial Ecosystems to Global Innovation Networks: Open Innovation, Double Networks, and Knowledge Integration," *International Journal of Entrepreneurship and Innovation Management* 14 (2011): 36–59.

13. J. V. Sinfield, E. Calder, B. McConnell, and S. Colson, "How to Identify New Business Models," *MIT Sloan Management Review* 53, no. 2 (Winter 2012): 85–90.

14. G. S. Day and P. J. Shoemaker, "Innovating in Uncertain Markets: 10 Lessons for Green Technologies," *MIT Sloan Management Review* 52, no. 4 (Summer 2011): 37–45.

15. N. Leiber, "Making the C in VC Stand for Corporate," *Bloomberg Businessweek*, July 4–10, 2011.

16. B. Stone, P. Burrows, and D. MacMillan, "I'll Take It from Here," *Bloomberg Businessweek.* January 31–February 6, 2011; D. Lyons, "Android Invasion," *Newsweek*, October 11, 2010, 32–37; B. Kowitt, "One Hundred Million Android Fans Can't Be Wrong," *Fortune*, July 4, 2011, 93–97.

17. P. F. Nunes and T. Breene, "Strategy at the Edge," *Accenture Outlook* (June 2011).

18. N. Radjou, J. Prabhu, and S. Ahuja, "What the West Can Learn from Jugaad," *Strategy and Business* 70 (November 19, 2012): 11–14.

19. J. R. Immelt, V. Govindarajan, and C. Trimble, "How GE Is Disrupting Itself," *Harvard Business Review* (October 2009): 3–11.

20. V. Sehgal, K. Dehoff, and G. Panneer, "The Importance of Frugal Engineering," *Strategy and Business* 59 (Summer 2010): 20–25.

21. B. Jaruzelski, J. Loehr, and R. Holman, "The Global Innovation 1000: Why Culture Is Key," *Strategy and Business* 65 (Winter 2011): 30–45.

CHAPTER 5: IMPLEMENTING THE STARTUP CORPORATION

1. R. Verganti, *Design-Driven Innovation: Changing the Rules of Competition by Radically Innovating What Things Mean* (Boston: Harvard Business Press, 2009).

2. T. Brown, *Change by Design: How Design Thinking Can Transform Organizations and Inspire Innovation* (New York: HarperCollins Publishers, 2009).

3. E. Von Hippel, *Democratizing Innovation* (Cambridge, MA: MIT Press, 2006).

4. W. C. Kim and R. Mauborgne, *Blue Ocean Strategy: How to Create Uncontested Market Space and Make Competition Irrelevant* (Boston: Harvard Business School Press, 2005).

5. For an analysis of how big data and other IT developments are changing the way businesses are run and innovation is managed, see E. Brynjolfsson, *Wired for Innovation: How Information Technology Is Reshaping the Economy* (Cambridge, MA: MIT Press, 2010).

6. For additional insights on stealth innovation, see P. Miller and T. Wedell-Wedellsborg, "The Case for Stealth Innovation," *Harvard Business Review* 91, no. 3 (March 2013): 90–97; and P. Miller and T. Wedell-Wedellsborg, *Innovation as Usual: How to Help Your People Bring Great Ideas to Life* (Boston: Harvard Business School Press, 2013).

7. P. Miller and T. Wedell-Wedellsborg, "Jordan Cohen at pfizerWorks: Building the Office of the Future," IESE Case DPO-187-E, 2010.

8. See S. Vossoughi, "Is the Social Sector Thinking Small Enough?," *Harvard Business Review* 89, no. 12 (December 2011): 40–41.

9. S. M. Datar and S. Chaturvedi, "BMVSS: Changing Lives, One Jaipur Limb at a Time," Harvard Business School Case 114007, 2013.

10. J. Lerner, *The Architecture of Innovation: The Economics of Creative Organizations* (Boston: Harvard Business Review Press, 2012).

11. L. Kolodny, "P&G Taps into Startups," *The Wall Street Journal*, February 2, 2013.

12. C. Markides and P. Geroski, *Fast Second: How Smart Companies Bypass Radical Innovation to Enter and Dominate New Markets* (San Francisco: Jossey-Bass, 2000).

13. H. W. Chesborough and A. R. Garman, "How Open Innovation Can Help You Cope in Lean Times," *Harvard Business Review* 87, no. 12 (2009): 68–76.

14. M. L. Tushman, W. K. Smith, and A. Binns, "The Ambidextrous CEO," *Harvard Business Review* 89, no. 6 (June 2011): 74–80.

15. F. Bidault and A. Castello, "Why Too Much Trust Is Death to Innovation," *MIT Sloan Management Review* 51, no. 4 (Summer 2010): 33–38.

16. A. Vance and C. C. Miller, "Google TV Faces Delays amid Poor Reviews," *The New York Times*, December 19, 2010.

17. "Companies & Industries," *Bloomberg Businessweek*, March 12–March 18, 2012.

18. K. Capell, "Novartis Radically Remaking Its Drug Business," *Businessweek*, June 22, 2009.

19. R. G. McGrath and I. C. Macmillan, *Discovery-Driven Growth: A Breakthrough Process to Reduce Risk and Seize Opportunity* (Boston: Harvard Business Review Press, 2009).

20. M. E. Porter, *Competitive Advantage: Techniques for Analyzing Industries and Competitors* (New York: Free Press, 1980); and A. Osterwalder and Y. Pigneur, *Business Model Generation: A Handbook for Visionaries, Game Changers, and Challengers* (Hoboken, NJ: John Wiley and Sons, 2010).

21. Brooks Barnes, "Disney Waves a High-Tech Wand over Its Stores," *The New York Times*, October 13, 2009.

22. Chesborough and Garman, "How Open Innovation Can Help You Cope in Lean Times."

CHAPTER 6: OVERCOMING THE INNOVATION PARADOX

1. C. K. Prahalad developed the concept of the bottom of the pyramid to refer to segments of the population with limited purchasing power but so large that in aggregate they form an attractive market. C. K. Prahalad and S. L. Hart, *The Fortune at the Bottom of the Pyramid* (Upper Saddle River, NJ: Prentice Hall, 2006).

2. For a description of play-to-win and play-not-to-lose, see T. Davila, M. J. Epstein, and R. Shelton, *Making Innovation Work: How to Manage It, Measure It, and Profit from It* (Upper Saddle River, NJ: Prentice Hall, 2013).

CHAPTER 7: INNOVATIVE CULTURES

1. For example, see J. P. Kotter and J. L. Heskett, *Corporate Culture and Performance* (New York: Free Press, 1992); and G. J. Tellis, *Unrelenting Innovation: How to Create a Culture for Market Dominance* (San Francisco: John Wiley and Sons, 2013).

2. R. Goffee and G. Jones, *The Character of a Corporation: How Your Company's Culture Can Make or Break Your Business* (London: Harper Collins Business, 1998), 15.

3. Aristotle, *The Nicomachean Ethics of Aristotle*, book 2, section 1, ed. W. D. Ross (Oxford: Oxford University Press, 1954).

4. For more details on Tesco, see J. F. Manzoni and J. L. Barsoux, "Tesco: Delivering the Goods (A) and (B)," IMD Case 3-1955, 3-1956, 2008.

5. Deloitte LLP, "Global Powers of Retailing 2013: Retail Beyond," http://www.deloitte.com/assets/Dcom-Australia/Local%20Assets/Documents/Industries/Consumer%20business/Deloitte_Global_Powers_of_Retail_2013.pdf.

6. Personal communication with Steve Jobs, D5 Conference: All Things Digital, May 30, 2007.

7. "Zappos Insights," http://www.zapposinsights.com/about/faqs.

8. T. Kelley, *The Art of Innovation: Lessons in Creativity from IDEO, America's Leading Design Firm* (New York: Random House, 2001).

9. E. Gardiner and C. J. Jackson, "Workplace Mavericks: How Personality and Risk-Taking Propensity Predicts Mavericism," *British Journal of Psychology* 103, no. 4 (2011): 497–519.

10. B. Stone, "Inside the Moonshot Factory: Google X's Silicon Valley Nerd Heaven—America's Last Great Corporate Research Lab," *Bloomberg Business Week*, May 22, 2013.

11. A. Vance, "Netflix, Reed Hastings Survive Missteps to Join Silicon Valley's Elite," *Businessweek*, May 9, 2009.

12. B. Jopson, "Ackman Attacks JC Penney Chief He Picked," *Financial Times*, April 5, 2013.

13. N. Cope, "The Monday Interview: Sir Terry Leahy," *The Independent*, March 25, 2002.

14. A. Lashinsky, "Amazon's Jeff Bezos: The Ultimate Disrupter," *Fortune*, November 16, 2012.

15. M. Reeves and M. Deimler, "Adaptability: The New Competitive Advantage," *Harvard Business Review* 89, no. 7 (July–August 2011): 135–141.

16. Lashinsky, "Amazon's Jeff Bezos."

17. J. F. Manzoni and J. L. Barsoux, *The Set Up to Fail Syndrome: How Good Managers Cause Great People to Fail* (Boston: Harvard Business School Press, 2002).

18. J. Clayton, B. Gambill, and D. Harned, "The Curse of Too Much Capital: Building New Businesses in Large Corporations," *McKinsey Quarterly* 3 (1999): 48–59.

CHAPTER 8: LEADING FOR BREAKTHROUGH INNOVATION

1. Along with the discussion of culture in chapter 7, this examination of leadership draws heavily on the ideas of Jean-François Manzoni, and we thank him for his insights and helpfulness.

2. "Performance Driver: Helmut Panke, Chief Executive, Bavarian Motor Works, Germany," *Businessweek*, June 7, 2004, 40.

3. CNN International.com, "In Focus, Lou Gerstner," http://edition.cnn .com/2004/BUSINESS/07/02/gerstner.interview/.

4. Forbes, "Steve Jobs: Get Rid of the Crappy Stuff," http://www.forbes .com/sites/carminegallo/2011/05/16/steve-jobs-get-rid-of-the-crappy -stuff/.

5. T. Davila, M. J. Epstein, and R. Shelton, *Making Innovation Work: How to Manage It, Measure It, and Profit from It* (Upper Saddle River, NJ: Prentice Hall, 2013).

6. C. Fishman, "Face Time with Michael Dell," *Fast Company*, February 28, 2001.

7. A. Lashinsky, "Amazon's Jeff Bezos: The Ultimate Disrupter," *Fortune*, November 16, 2010.

8. Ibid.

9. A. Grove, *Only the Paranoid Survive: How to Exploit the Crisis Points That Challenge Every Company* (New York: Random House, 1996).

10. A. Higginson, "Interview: Andrew Higginson, Finance and Strategy Director, Tesco," *Financial Management*, March 1, 2005, 6.

11. J. Riera, "Scaling Great Heights," *Retail Week*, April 8, 2005, 5.

12. J. Schwartz, "Dell Computer Is in the Catbird Seat, for Now," *The New York Times*, September 11, 2001.

13. P. Hemp, "Managing for the Next Big Thing: An Interview with Michael Ruettgers," *Harvard Business Review* 79, no. 1 (January 2001): 130–139.
14. Lou Gerstner, quoted in *Business Life* (May 2000): 16.
15. C. Gallo, *The Innovation Secrets of Steve Jobs: Insanely Different Principles for Breakthrough Success* (New York: McGraw-Hill, 2011), 221.
16. A. Park and P. Burrows, "What You Don't Know about Dell," *Businessweek*, November 2, 2003.
17. A. L. Tucker and S. J. Singer, "Key Drivers of Successful Implementation of an Employee Suggestion–Driven Improvement Program," Harvard Business School Working Paper no. 12-112, 2012.
18. Conversation with Bill Gates, D5 Conference, 2007, http://allthingsd.com/20070531/d5-gates-jobs-transcript/.
19. B. Stone, "Inside the Moonshot Factory: Google X's Silicon Valley Nerd Heaven—America's Last Great Corporate Research Lab," *Bloomberg Business Week*, May 22, 2013.
20. George S. Patton, quoted in Gallo, *The Innovation Secrets of Steve Jobs*, 219.
21. S. Wozniak and G. Smith, *iWoz: Computer Geek to Cult Icon: How I Invented the Personal Computer, Co-Founded Apple, and Had Fun Doing It* (New York: W. W. Norton & Company, 2006), 289.

CHAPTER 9: HARD FOUNDATIONS

1. This discussion dates back to the concept of hygiene factors: see F. Herzberg, *Work and the Nature of Man* (Oxford: World Publishing, 1966); see also M. C. Jensen, *Theory of the Firm: Governance, Residual Claims, and Organizational Forms* (Cambridge, MA: Harvard University Press, 2000); and A. Kohn, "Why Incentive Plans Cannot Work," *Harvard Business Review* 71, no. 5 (September–October 1993): 54–63. For a discussion of economic incentives, see J. Lerner, *The Architecture of Innovation: The Economics of Creative Organizations* (Boston: Harvard Business Review Press, 2012).
2. J. Hempel, "IBM's Super Second Act," *Fortune*, March 21, 2011, 115–124.
3. S. Lohr, "Apple and I.B.M. Aren't All That Different," *The New York Times*, November 6, 2010.
4. C. K. Prahalad and R. A. Mashelkar, "Innovation's Holy Grail," *Harvard Business Review* 88, no. 7 (July–August 2010): 132–141.
5. A. Wooldridge, "Where Innovation Runs Deep," *Korn/Ferry Briefings* (Spring 2011).
6. V. Sehgal, K. Dehoff, and G. Panneer, "The Importance of Frugal Engineering," *Strategy and Business* 59 (Summer 2010): 20–25.
7. K. Capell, "Novartis Radically Remaking Its Drug Business," *Businessweek*, June 22, 2009.
8. B. Jaruzelski and K. Dehoff, "How the Top Innovators Keep Winning," *Strategy and Business* 61 (Winter 2010): 48.

9. R. Walker, "Jeff Bezos, Amazon.com," April 1, 2004, http://www.inc .com/magazine/20040401/25bezos.html.

10. G. Kawasaki, "Ten Commandments from an Entrepreneurial 'Evangelist,'" Knowledge@Wharton, June 10, 2009.

11. R. Simons, *Levers of Control: How Managers Use Innovative Control Systems to Drive Strategic Renewal* (Boston: Harvard Business School Press, 1995).

12. "Akio Morita: Gadget Guru," October 9, 2008, http://www.entrepreneur .com/article/197676#.

13. S. Johnson, "On the Inside, Looking Out," *CFO* 27, no. 2 (March 2011): 21–24.

14. S. Cook, "The Contribution Revolution: Letting Volunteers Build Your Business," *Harvard Business Review* 86, no. 10 (October 2008): 60–69.

15. A. Lashinsky, "The Secrets Apple Keeps," *Fortune*, February 6, 2012, 85–94.

16. G. Emmons, J. Hanna, and R. Thompson, "Five Ways to Make Your Company More Innovative," *Harvard Business School Working Knowledge*, May 23, 2012.

17. V. Govindarajan and C. Timble, "The CEO's Role in Business Model Reinvention," *Harvard Business Review* (January–February 2011): 109–114.

18. T. Davila, M. J. Epstein, and R. Shelton, *Making Innovation Work: How to Manage It, Measure It, and Profit from It* (Upper Saddle River, NJ: Prentice Hall, 2013).

INDEX

ABOUT THE AUTHORS

Tony Davila heads the Entrepreneurship and Innovation Center as well as the entrepreneurship department at IESE Business School in Barcelona, where he also is a professor in the accounting and control department. He teaches courses in innovation management, entrepreneurship, management accounting and control, and  sports management at the master, doctoral, and executive education levels. During 2013, he was the MBA Class of 1961 Visiting Professor at Harvard Business School. Previously, he was a faculty member at the Graduate School of Business, Stanford University, after receiving his doctorate from Harvard Business School. He has taught innovation and entrepreneurship around the world, including at Oxford University in England, HEC Lausanne in Switzerland, and CEIBS in China.

Dr. Davila is the coauthor of *Making Innovation Work: How to Manage It, Measure It, and Profit from It* (2006, 2013) and *Performance Measurement and Management Control Systems to Implement Strategy* (2000). He also is the coauthor of *Malea Fashion District:*

How Successful Managers Use Financial Information to Grow Organizations (2009, 2012). In addition, he edited *The Creative Enterprise* (2007). He is a prolific author of teaching cases with companies such as Checkpoint, Logitech, FC Barcelona, Siebel Systems, CitiBank, and Salesforce.com.

His work has been published in diverse journals, including *Harvard Business Review, California Management Review, Journal of Business Venturing,* and *Research Policy.* He has received IESE's research award three times, and his dissertation was distinguished by the American Accounting Association. His latest article in *California Management Review* received the Accenture Best Paper Award, 2010. He was also a finalist for the McKinsey Best Paper Award from the Strategic Management Society. The Spanish government awarded him the Ramón y Cajal scholarship for his work.

Dr. Davila serves as an advisor and consultant to companies in Europe and North and South America, ranging from large multinationals to venture-backed startups.

Marc J. Epstein is Distinguished Research Professor of Management at Jones Graduate School of Business at Rice University in Houston. Prior to joining Rice, he was a professor at Stanford Business School, Harvard Business School, and INSEAD (European Institute of Business Administration). In both academic research and  managerial practice, Dr. Epstein is considered one of the global leaders in the areas of innovation, sustainability, governance, performance measurement, and accountability in corporations as well as not-for-profit organizations.

Dr. Epstein has extensive academic and practical experience in the implementation of corporate strategies and the development of performance metrics for use in these implementations. He has been a senior consultant to leading corporations and governments throughout the world for more than twenty-five years. His many recent articles and books detail how the use of new strategic management systems can help companies focus strategy, link to performance metrics, and drive improved performance.

He has worked with eminent global companies on improving their incremental and breakthrough business models and technology innovation. He also has published widely on developing processes to improve organizational performance and on the measurement of success. His coauthored book *Making Innovation Work: How to Manage It, Measure It, and Profit from It* (2006, 2013) has had worldwide use.

In addition, Dr. Epstein is currently working in developing countries in Africa, Asia, and South America on innovative and entrepreneurial solutions to global challenges and measuring and managing the social impacts of corporations, NGOs, and foundations. Each year he takes all of his MBA students to Africa as part of his course "Commercializing Technology in Developing Countries." In 2013, his book *Pharmacy on a Bicycle: Innovative Solutions for Global Health and Poverty* was released.

His twenty authored or coauthored books and more than two hundred professional papers have won numerous top academic, professional, and business awards.

Berrett–Koehler
Publishers

Berrett–Koehler
Publishers

A community dedicated to creating
a world that works for all

Dear Reader,

Thank you for picking up this book and joining our worldwide community of Berrett-Koehler readers. We share ideas that bring positive change into people's lives, organizations, and society.

To welcome you, we'd like to offer you a free e-book. You can pick from among twelve of our bestselling books by entering the promotional code BKP92E here: http://www.bkconnection.com/welcome.

When you claim your free e-book, we'll also send you a copy of our e-newsletter, the *BK Communiqué*. Although you're free to unsubscribe, there are many benefits to sticking around. In every issue of our newsletter you'll find

- A free e-book
- Tips from famous authors
- Discounts on spotlight titles
- Hilarious insider publishing news
- A chance to win a prize for answering a riddle

Best of all, our readers tell us, "Your newsletter is the only one I actually read." So claim your gift today, and please stay in touch!

Sincerely,

Charlotte Ashlock
Steward of the BK Website

Questions? Comments? Contact me at bkcommunity@bkpub.com.

Certified

Corporation
bcorporation.net